Betsy Sikora Siino

Samoyeds

Everything about Purchase, Care, Nutrition, Grooming, Behavior, and Training

With 55 Color Photographs

Illustrations by Tana Hakanson

BARRON'S

© Copyright 1998 by Barron's Educational Series, Inc.

All rights reserved.

No part of this book may be reproduced in any form by photostat, microfilm, xerography, or any other means, or incorporated into any information retrieval system, electronic or mechanical, without the written permission of the copyright owner.

All inquiries should be addressed to:
Barron's Educational Series, Inc.
250 Wireless Boulevard
Hauppauge, NY 11788

International Standard Book No. 0-7641-0175-7

Library of Congress Catalog Card No. 97-40515

Library of Congress Cataloging-in-Publication Data
Siino, Betsy Sikora.
　　Samoyeds : everything about purchase, care, nutrition, breeding, behavior, and training / Betsy Sikora Siino ; illustrations by Tana Hakanson.
　　　　p.　　cm.
　　Includes bibliographical references (p. 108) and index.
　　ISBN 0-7641-0175-7
　　1. Samoyed dog. I. Title.
　　SF429.S35S55　　1998
　　636.73—dc21
　　　　　　　　　　　　　　　　　　　　97-40515
　　　　　　　　　　　　　　　　　　　　CIP

Printed in Hong Kong

987654321

About the Author
Betsy Sikora Siino is an award-winning writer of books (*You Want a What For A Pet?!*, *Dogs on the Web*, and *The Siberian Husky*) and articles, primarily on subjects related to animals. Her most recent book, *Alaskan Malamutes*, was published by Barron's Educational Series in 1997. As former staff writer for *Dog Fancy*, *Dogs USA*, *Pet Health News*, *and Horse Illustrated* magazines, she has a special affinity for horses, wildlife, and, most of all, for dogs, particularly for the great northern breeds (the Alaskan Malamute, the Samoyed, the American Eskimo, and the Siberian Husky among them). A graduate of the University of California at Davis, Betsy is a member of the Author's Guild and the Dog Writers Association of America (from which she was awarded Maxwell Medallions for her work on wolf/dog hybrids and wild canids). She has a special interest in subjects related to wild species and their survival, and has received acclaim for her work on wolves, coyotes, and other wild predators, as well as on such controversial issues as the Endangered Species Act and the preservation of wild lands.

Important Note
This pet owner's guide tells the reader how to buy and care for a Samoyed. The author and the publisher consider it important to point out that the advice given in the book is meant primarily for normally developed puppies from a good breeder—that is, dogs of excellent physical health and good character.

Anyone who adopts a fully grown dog should be aware that the animal has already formed its basic impressions of human beings. The new owner should watch the animal carefully, including its behavior toward humans, and should meet the previous owner. If the dog comes from a shelter, it may be possible to get some information on the dog's background and peculiarities there. There are dogs that, as a result of bad experiences with humans, behave in an unnatural manner or may even bite. Only people that have experience with dogs should take in such animals.

Caution is further advised in the association of children with dogs, in meeting with other dogs, and in exercising the dog without a leash.

Even well-behaved and carefully supervised dogs sometimes do damage to someone else's property or cause accidents. It is therefore in the owner's interest to be adequately insured against such eventualities, and we strongly urge all dog owners to purchase a liability policy that covers their dog.

Contents

Acknowledgments

Since childhood I have studied rigorously the vocations and characteristics of the world's many dog breeds, one of my favorites being the Samoyed. I am thus both honored and privileged to have been offered the opportunity to write this book and to make my own contribution to the rich body of literature that has been produced about this illustrious animal. I hope that my words will serve not only to assist owners in the care and nurturing of the Samoyed, but also help to improve the public's overall understanding of and respect for the Samoyed.

For this once-in-a-lifetime opportunity, I must thank my dedicated, dog-

The headstrong, often demanding Samoyed is not the appropriate pet for every household, but for those individuals who are drawn to the breed for pure and realistic reasons, there is no finer companion.

loving editors at Barron's who value the writer's body of knowledge as well as her voice. Grace Freedson, I thank you for entrusting me with your beloved Marshmallow's breed. Mary Falcon, I thank and appreciate you more than you can know for shepherding the book through a rigorous editorial process that has resulted in a lovely finished product.

Also in need of thanks are the countless Samoyed breeders, rescuers, veterinarians, and trainers with whom I have come in contact through the years. In regard to this particular project, I extend special thanks to the ladies of Samoyed Rescue of Southern California—Lory Barra, Susan Whitecotton, and Barbara Arnaud—for sharing with me their abundant Sammy knowledge. Also deserving of my gratitude are internationally renowned Samoyed enthusiasts, Kent and Donna Dannen, who have for years inspired me and the public at large with their photographs of Sams at work, at play, and at everything in between. I am most honored that some of their breathtaking images are gracing the pages of this book, which simply would not have been complete without their contributions.

Never to be forgotten, of course, is my family. I thank my parents, Robert and Louise Sikora, for instilling and fostering in me a profound love for the canine species that runs deep in our clan. And I thank those who remain patient with me day in and day out as I heed my innate drive to fiddle with words on the computer: Michael, Christopher, and the now rather elderly canine member of our family, Rebel. You guys know I couldn't do it without you.

4

Introduction

A Universal Smile—The Samoyed

One of my earliest and most vivid childhood memories revolves around my delight at scouring over and over again a large book of dog breeds that my parents gave me when I was still a toddler. Today, on those occasions when I take that treasured volume, now so tattered and torn, from the bookshelf, I can distinctly remember the joy that would course through me as I lovingly turned each page. The images on those pages quickly became as familiar to me as old friends, but there was one I found particularly enticing. Presented on that page, against a sparkling backdrop of snow and ice, was the image of a beautiful dog with a thick white coat, a lush tail that curled up over its back, and a smile on its face that made its beauty accessible to all who happened to browse through the book. That dog was, of course, the Samoyed.

Through the years I have been faced with countless more such images, and even now they never cease to melt my heart. I often wonder if it was the Samoyed's influence on my childhood, conveyed through the lovely painting on a page of what would be the first of many volumes in a rather large canine library, that steered the course my life would take as a journalist specializing in

Portrait of a Samoyed father and son.

the subject of dogs. Such influence would not be unheard of. Through my many years of experiences with dogs, I have witnessed personally the Samoyed's magic, a magic sprung from the breed's glacial home at the top of the world, a magic that is universal in scope.

I recall receiving a letter one day at my office during the Persian Gulf War when I was staff writer for *Dog Fancy* magazine—one of the few publications approved for Desert Storm reading. The letter was from a 19-year-old marine then stationed in Saudi Arabia. He was writing in response to an article I had written about Tundra, a gorgeous, multi-talented Samoyed of television and movie fame, who was prominently featured in *Communicating With Your Dog,* an unforgettable training book, another Barron's title,

written by Tundra's owner Ted Baer. The young man, upon reading the article, felt compelled to write and convey to me how much this piece, and this beautiful dog, had brightened what was truly a terrifying experience for him. Comforted by Tundra's presence on the page, her smiling face and obvious sense of humor, he was able to confide the depth of his fear to a stranger to whom he felt linked by a mutual love and respect for a beautiful white dog. In the end, I think he emerged just a little less frightened, a little less uncertain about his situation.

The tears still fill my eyes when I read that letter, and I can't help but reflect on all the other people of differing backgrounds and circumstances throughout the centuries whose lives the Samoyed has brightened with its smile. From the Samoyed people who were helped by these friendly white dogs to survive in one of the most hostile regions on the planet; to explorers who led expeditions to the polar ice caps, perhaps allowing their dogs and only their dogs to see their fear; to a lonely child in a contemporary American household in need of the support the Samoyed is expert in providing, all understand the universal admiration and gratitude expressed by that frightened young soldier stationed in a desert thousands of miles from his home. All have been touched by the magic of the Samoyed, a canine guardian angel who will no doubt continue to touch our species with this same special magic for thousands of years to come.

Getting to Know Samoyeds

Imagine for a moment that you are lost on the frozen tundra of Siberia. It is mid-winter. You have no way of knowing whether it is day or night, for the sun never shows its face. You no longer feel your feet, your fingers, your ears. As the bitter cold grips your brain, a gentle wave of soft euphoria begins to flow through your consciousness. You are in grave danger.

Suddenly you hear something. You look off to the horizon. An apparition approaches. Glowing in the darkness, an unknown light glistening off pristine silver-tipped coats of fur, they come closer. And closer. Barking—yes, that is the sound. They are dogs, the most beautiful dogs you have ever seen. They must be angels, guardian angels sent to your rescue.

But these dogs are not angels. They are not apparitions. They are living, breathing creatures harnessed to a sled and driven by a fur-shrouded musher. Across this brutal landscape that has claimed countless lives, they run with joyful abandon to greet you, their mouths curved collectively into the smile for which these beautiful dogs have become legendary. The dogs are Samoyeds, and they and their partnership with this, their homeland, can legitimately claim the title of unsung eighth wonder of the world.

For the Love of Man

Of course, in reality you are not lost in the Arctic in need of rescue by a team of smiling Samoyeds, and frankly, Sammies no longer pull sleds across Siberia for people who rely on them for their very existence. For centuries, however, these dogs did just that, and for centuries they lived as beautiful treasures amid what might otherwise be considered nothing but a wasteland, devoid of any ability to sustain life. But because of the Samoyed, this region did sustain life—and it brought along an extra bonus as well, in the form of an incredible dog that

Together, the Samoyed people and their beautiful smiling white dogs carved out a rugged existence in the Siberian Arctic for hundreds of years.

An ancient, very natural breed, the Samoyed is almost unreal in its breathtaking beauty and genuine affection for the human species.

The noble Samoyed, with its dignity, humor, loving demeanor, and tireless work ethic, has through history earned the loyalty of all whose lives it has touched.

survived to bring its extraordinary gifts into our contemporary homes today.

That incredible dog called the top of the world home for thousands of years. Considered one of the oldest breeds of dog, all we know of the Samoyed's past is that for those millenia, isolated as it was within the northwestern region of Siberia in the Arctic Circle, it bred pure and true for more generations than we will ever know. Only the seminomadic Samoyed people of ages past, the tribe from whom this lovely white dog takes its name, were privy to the Samoyed's evolutionary tale. We do not know where the Samoyed came from, nor do we know when it landed on the ice of its Arctic home. All we know is that the hardy souls that would be the Samoyed's benefactors could never have survived had it not been for their dogs.

Faced with life on a frozen, dangerously barren, landscape, the Samoyed people had only their dogs and their reindeer to help them carve out an existence in this seemingly godforsaken region. They would herd the reindeer, hunt what game they could, and live in portable leather tents called *chooms* that they could transport from place to place. What is remarkable is the way in which this lifestyle dovetailed with the harsh climate and terrain of their Siberian home, to sculpt the Samoyed, a dog of such prowess, such wit, such beauty, and such affection for the human species.

A Dog of Contradictions and Versatility

The Samoyed is very much a dog of contradictions. Yes, the Sammy was sprung from the cruelest and most treacherous region on the planet, yet it is a beautiful, effervescent, joyful animal, and, from what little we know of its primitive past, it always has been. Yes, the Samoyed resembles an irresistible stuffed toy that demands attention from passersby, yet what may come as a surprise to those passersby is the fact that it also happens to be a tireless and multitalented worker. Historically, it had to be, or it, and its people, would perish.

Of all the northern dog breeds—the Alaskan Malamute, the Siberian Husky, the Greenland Dog—the Samoyed is the most versatile. Necessity dictated that it possess a herding instinct to keep the reindeer in line, that it be somewhat adept at hunting to accompany its people on forays for food, that it sport a lush protective coat and efficient metabolism to withstand the rigors of Arctic life, and that it be strong enough to pull sledges across the ice as its family moved from place to place. But somewhere along the line the Samoyed also developed a legendary love for the human species. One look into its smiling eyes, and you'll see the many generations of Samoyed people who welcomed their beloved white canine namesakes into their chooms for their nightly slumber, the dogs' warmth all that stood between a family freezing to death in the night and awakening in the morning to greet a new day.

Indeed, it is the Samoyed's profound, people-loving temperament that stands out most prominently in this dog, even surpassing its great beauty and the stunning white coat that itself seems an extension of the sparkling ice of the dog's homeland. Living in such close quarters for thousands of years couldn't help but foster a special closeness between the Samoyed people and their dogs, a closeness that was especially profound between the dogs and the children of the family.

An Indelible Bond

We actually know very little about the Samoyed people, but the nature of their dogs offers clues to their charac-

A beloved member of the family even within its native land, the Samoyed has long harbored a special affinity for children.

ter that rival those that might be found in even the richest archeological excavation. Some Arctic breeds, the Greenland Dog and Eskimo Dog, among them, have reputations for being wild, aloof, even fierce in character, thanks to their people who viewed them solely in a utilitarian light and treated them accordingly. The jubilant character of today's Samoyed, however, stands as a testament to the relatively kind and respectful treatment this breed has received through the ages. Perhaps its people knew innately what contemporary studies have proven about the magic of the human/animal bond. Perhaps they understood that the Samoyed—the beauty, the clown, the loving companion—could, with its smile and encouraging nature, help fend off the inevitable sense of doom and despair that could creep into a dark choom during an endless Arctic winter night.

In their wisdom, it would seem the Samoyed people chose to trust their dogs' instincts on the job and bestow them with full-fledged family membership at home. The result is seen in

Sammies today in the almost clairvoyant relationship they share with their contemporary families. The look of belonging in the Samoyed's eyes is unmistakable when you walk into a home that contains one of these animals. The dog belongs with this clan, it seems to say. You may rest assured that that animal is also profoundly sensitive to the interactions within its household—particularly when family members argue, which can be very upsetting for the sensitive Sam who seeks harmony in all its daily life.

Chalk up this miraculous and very mutual relationship to the fact that the Samoyed was called upon for millennia to perform a variety of tasks that required a canine partner that could think and reason. The breed thus developed a sensibility that made it almost human in its partnership with the two-legged creatures in its midst. Or attribute the dog's great beauty and sense of humor for inspiring the relatively benevolent care it invited and received.

Yet, despite the special bond the Samoyed forged with its native families, life was anything but a breeze in the Siberian Arctic. This region presented daily a true test of the theory of survival of the fittest, and while the breed as a whole lived to claim victory over the elements, many a dog was lost in this vicious process. Food was scarce and probably offered sporadically. The work demands were unrelenting and the temperatures subzero. Only the strongest survived, and only the strongest were bestowed with the high honor, not only of sharing the warmth and camaraderie within their peoples' chooms after a day of heavy toil, but of procreating, as well.

The Turning Point

Despite the great challenges sent their way, many a Samoyed prevailed, and, thanks to the often cruel stroke of Mother Nature's sculpting knife, the cream of the Arctic's best-kept secret survived to greet the twentieth century. Indeed, in this century the Samoyed would make a revolutionary entrance onto the canine scene.

It would be the Samoyed's ample physical talents and work ethic that would propel it to world fame—and not, as one would think, only its great beauty. This began in the late 1800s when Norwegian explorer and Nobel Prize winner Fridtjof Nansen began to plan an excursion to the North Pole. He decided, correctly, of course, that the best way to traverse this frozen land would be by dogsled. Next step: Find the right dogs.

Rumor had it, thanks to a smattering of explorers who had ventured into the forbidding area, that the nomadic people of Siberia lived among a race of extraordinary dogs with coats as white as the snow of their native landscape, dogs whose muscle, strength, and intelligence were the best insurance for a safe and effective journey, and whose friendly natures would make that journey all the more pleasant. Needless to say, it was these dogs, Samoyeds, that were called upon to guide Nansen's expedition.

From then on, the wheels were set in motion. The hunger to explore the poles became an epidemic, and adventurers from all nations caught the fever. They also paid close attention to Nansen's experience, and sought to recruit Samoyeds for their own expeditions, as well. But it was Norwegian explorer Roald Amundsen's successful attempt to reach the South Pole in 1911, a 1,860-mile (2,993 km) round trip that took 99 days, that would ultimately propel the Samoyed's name into the headlines worldwide. Indeed, the first animal to reach the Pole was a Samoyed, and from then on, its fate was sealed.

Many of the courageous expedition Samoyeds never made it back alive from their polar travels, most of them meeting bleak ends on the ice as vital though expendable casualties of man's desire for immortality. But those that did survive found a welcoming crowd awaiting them. Not only were the dogs consummate adventurers and athletes, but they were exquisitely beautiful. Some actually ended up on display in zoos in Britain and Australia, while others would become the foundation of the breeding programs that would become the contemporary core of this breed throughout the world.

Virtually every Samoyed among us today—pet, show dog, sled dog alike—is a descendant of the dynamic dogs that joined the various and sundry assaults on the North and South Poles. This fact alone accounts for the Samoyed's reputation as such a hardy breed, for these expeditions, as harsh and unforgiving as they were, once again challenged this dog to emerge victorious in natural selection's battle for the survival of the fittest.

At the turn of the twentieth century, the Samoyed became a favored accessory for those of royal, aristocratic, and similarly wealthy backgrounds.

An Illustrious Century

Once a fixture in what we might call civilization, the Samoyed settled down into a less treacherous lifestyle. So ensconced, it was now able to follow its desire for human company without the danger of losing its life to cold, starvation, or other threats. In the past 100 years, this dog has undergone a transition from expedition vehicle to cherished pet, popular show dog, and recreational sled dog. The Samoyed proved instantly to be a natural for the gentler callings of twentieth-century life, and has taken to its new role quite readily.

England was the country where the Sammy first made a splash, imported and promoted there by enthusiasts Mr. and Mrs. Ernest Kilburn-Scott. The public soon learned that though this dog had traversed the wilds of the polar ice caps and lived to bark about it, it was just as loving and gentle as the teddy-bear image it conveyed.

Not surprisingly, the Samoyed also became the immediate recipient of royal patronage, enjoying the devotion of, among others, England's King Edward VII and the ill-fated household of Russia's Czar Nicholas and his empress Alexandra, who became much enamored of this treasure from their own Siberian backyard. Nothing enhanced photographs, architecture, interior design, and other trappings of wealth and position more dramatically than the lush, pristine white fur, the dark twinkling eyes, and the loving smile of the Samoyed. That is as true today as it was almost 100 years ago.

Bred as sled dog for both the native Samoyed people and polar expeditions, the Samoyed continues to carry on this vocational tradition today.

Arrival in the United States

While the Samoyed's cousins, the larger, heavier Alaskan Malamute and the smaller, quicker Siberian Husky, made their way into the lower 48 in answer to the demand for sled dogs to feed the growing recreational mushing rage, the equally talented Sam's arrival had more to do with its pet characteristics than its athletic prowess. The first recorded Samoyeds to land on American soil did so when they accompanied yet another royal personage to this country: Belgium's Princess de Montyglyon, an heiress to the Holy Roman Empire, in 1904. It was one of her dogs that was the first Samoyed to be registered by the American Kennel Club in 1906. From then on, the breed gained a steady following. This resulted in the founding of the Samoyed Club of America in 1923, which helped guide American breeding efforts and convinced enthusiasts that this dog must be nurtured

and preserved so it might carry on for thousands of years more in its very pure, very pristine, very lovable state.

Today's Samoyed

While the Samoyed has enjoyed a steady growth in both numbers and identity through the decades of the twentieth century, it has remained very much the same in appearance and temperament as the native Sams of Siberia. Improvements in diet, grooming, and living conditions have resulted in larger Samoyeds with lusher coats —and longer life spans. This is a natural dog that remains so to this day. And fortunately, most people who have been attracted to this breed have pledged their allegiance to maintaining its natural gifts.

Today the smiling face of the Samoyed remains a favorite among dog people and non-dog people alike. It is a natural artist's model, a delightful photographer's muse, and its loose hair can even be harvested and spun into a unique and very beautiful yarn. On the more commercially oriented art scene, this breed remains a favorite accessory for models in fashion spreads and magazine advertisement layouts. One would imagine, however, that the models would rebel against sharing the page with a dog that would surely outshine them in beauty and charisma. The same can be said of the Samoyeds whose smiling faces have been featured in movies and on television, calling to mind the old adage that an actor should, if at all possible, avoid sharing the stage with children and animals. Forget the kids. Forget the other animals. The Samoyed will upstage them all.

The Samoyed Smile

Another phenomenon that has followed the Samoyed throughout its contemporary history, is the tendency among those who behold this dog to equate it automatically with the spirit of Christmas. It's the smile that does it.

Sometimes referred to as "the dog with Christmas on its face," you can almost imagine Kris Kringle mushing a team of smiling white Sammies between his workshop and the main house, the dogs, white marshmallows of fur, smiling in unison as they revel in their responsibilities—the North Pole, as those turn-of-the-century explorers obviously suspected, is, after all, this dog's home turf.

But today, anywhere and everywhere is the Samoyed's home turf. It may be found across all oceans, within all borders. Wherever there are people to love and to share a mutual respect is home to the Samoyed. And as long as these people understand and respect the Sam's need for daily activity, its insatiable sense of humor, and its headstrong, even free-thinking intelligence, the relationship is destined for success.

Whether one chooses to pronounce this dog's name as Sam-oy-yed, Sam-a-yed, or Sammy-yed, whether it is enlisted for a sled dog team or simply as a family member involved in every single activity of the day, the Sammy's concern is the commitment and the camaraderie that was bred into this dog over thousands of years of isolation in the ice and snow of Siberia. Truly an example of "the fittest," having been sculpted by nature's chisel with a little help from humankind, this dog seems an unexplained gift to the earth from some unknown, but obviously very generous, deity with a passion for life on the ice.

So, though Samoyeds may not be angelic entities in the classic, winged sense, many an owner views them as

Even at only a few weeks of age, Sammy puppies are most at home in the snow and ice.

earthbound angels, for to them, life with a Samoyed is heaven. Life without one...well, suffice it to say that a life sans Sammy for these individuals evokes images of that other place.

Choosing a Samoyed Companion

Why a Samoyed?

If you think that the lovely facade and even lovelier internal character of the Samoyed must surely make this dog the perfect pet for all people, think again. Yes, this dog is a delightful, not to mention beautiful, presence around the house, but only those who truly understand its soul, its energy, and its ample ownership requirements need apply.

You see, the handling and maintenance of the Samoyed requires a great deal of preparation, effort, and skill. Consider that great white coat, for instance. While it is indeed natural to this dog, it requires constant grooming to keep it free of mats, parasites, and overgrowth. The Sammy mind, too, though gentle and loving to the core, can lead this dog down the path to trouble—destructive and dangerous behavior—if its energies are not targeted every single day in positive directions via firm, yet humane, methods.

The underlying message here is clear: In most cases, the Samoyed is not appropriate for first-time dog owners, or for dog owners who are not adequately prepared or motivated to devote themselves 100 percent to the grand responsibility of dog care. From the moment this dog crosses its new threshold, the subsequent success of the relationship hinges on your commitment to working daily to help the Sam understand its place in the household, its boundaries, its training, and its routine. In the Samoyed you will find a willing, though sometimes headstrong, student, so address the animal with respect, let it know who is boss (you), and you will ultimately gain entrance to a special world only Sammy owners understand.

Entering that world requires a great deal more than simply spotting the irresistible mug of a teddy-bear-adorable Sammy pup, falling in love, and bringing your new love home. As with any dog, this is a lifelong commitment. That precious little bundle will soon grow into a beautiful, smiling animal of 55 pounds (25 kg) or more with a heavy coat of white hair and a desire to play, exercise, and commune with its family that simply must be satisfied. Training, too, will be a challenge, for this dog boasts an ancient intelligence that has for millennia dictated that it think for itself or die on the ice.

So, bringing that new little Sammy puppy home is only the beginning; you then face a mountain of often very frustrating work ahead of you. But do your homework ahead of time, learn about the inner workings of this dog's mind, choose your new pet wisely, and you will be rewarded. Though at times you will wonder why and how you ever got involved with this often exasperating animal, you may come to realize what so many before you have—from Siberia to Australia, from the Arctic to the South Pole, from England to Russia to North America and beyond—that life simply isn't as enchanting, as fulfilling, as just plain fun, without a Samoyed around the house.

The Samoyed's Wish List

Most Samoyeds have a very difficult time keeping secrets. If they have a thought or opinion or desire, they will work very hard to convey that message to their special people. They will chortle and warble and whimper—they have quite a vocabulary. If that doesn't get your attention, they will resort to Sammy sign language, an innate paw-driven language that seems to be passed on genetically from one generation of Sams to the next.

While most owners in time learn to interpret what their pets are trying to tell them in Sam language, it's a safe bet that they will never be privy to all the nuances obviously entailed in a language spoken by dogs of such ancient lineage. For example, were we to inquire into just what the Samoyed is looking for in an owner, it's an even safer bet that this dog, though devoted most democratically to the human species as a whole, would offer up a rather complete list of wishes.

This dog comes into its new home with a roster of demands that it simply assumes will be met as part of the covenant between itself and its new family. In addition to the standard wishes for good food (but not so much of it as to lead to obesity), fresh water, routine vaccinations, and regular grooming, the Samoyed demands full and unequivocal family membership, an expectation that is genetically programmed into this dog's DNA.

Family membership. In the Arctic the Sam enjoyed this family-member status and in return accepted its people into the family of dogs. All must be mutual for this dog, so, when you invite a Samoyed into the family, you adopt that dog in the purest sense of the word and you will find yourself adopted in exchange—this dog simply cannot understand or abide any other existence. While this may seem a given to many a pet owner, some people may find such a commitment annoying or unattainable, so think about this before bringing a Samoyed into the household.

Attention. Hand in hand with that card-carrying family membership is the attention the Samoyed will demand from its family. Any activity in which the family is participating, whether it be a game of baseball in the park, a backyard barbecue, spring cleaning in the garage, or even building a bookshelf for the living room, the Samoyed will insist on being right smack in the heart of the action. Relegate the dog to another room and you will hear about it until you relent and allow the dog the involvement it so heartily demands.

Need for exercise. Commensurate with that attention requirement is the Sammy's need for exercise, daily exercise. If you choose to ignore this important element of Sammy care, one borne of thousands of years of tireless athletic activity for survival in the Arctic, you will end up with a dog that is bored, destructive, incessantly barky, and probably overweight as well. You need not take daily excursions across the tundra by dogsled, but make sure that each day the dog is allowed to accompany you on a walk, a jog, or

Despite its irresistible appearance and demeanor, a new Samoyed puppy must be chosen with the head as well as the heart.

The Samoyed's innate desire to spend hours in the snow on a cold winter's day is just one of the many wishes the dog will make clear to its owners.

any energy-expending activity that exercises the dog's mind as well as its body. Your Sam will in turn live long, prosper, and probably decide not to use the legs

The Samoyed will demand to play an integral role in every family activity.

of the antique dining room table for chew toys.

Bringing any dog into the family can alter the entire rhythm of the household, but this is especially true when that dog is one that requires an owner's commitment to athletic endeavor. Neither rain nor sleet nor snow nor dark of night shall keep the responsible Sammy's owner from his or her appointed responsibilities to the dog. It's raining? Too bad. The dog must go out. Snowing? Even better. Just don't fight it. Accept this as a very positive responsibility of dog ownership and enjoy.

Intangibles. Rounding out the Samoyed's owner wish list are the intangibles. Given its choice, the smiling Sam would gladly choose a family with a sense of humor that will keep it smiling and chortling as only a Sammy can do all year round. But don't worry—even the most stoic of owners will soon be smiling once a Samoyed joins the household. More contagious than a nursery-school cold is the Sammy sense of humor.

Be warned, too, that the classic Samoyed may also have strong, again genetically imprinted, opinions about where it wishes to sleep at night. Think back again to those native Sams that were accustomed to sharing their owner's chooms. Many a Sam today strives to carry on that tradition, happiest to sleep on its owner's bed—or at least beside it. Such an arrangement can come in handy during a cold winter night when you're trying to economize on the heating bill.

What to Look For

Once you have deemed that you are worthy of life with the Samoyed—and have thus educated yourself all you can about this lovely breed—the next logical step is to determine what to look for in a Samoyed you hope will share the next 12 to 15 years of your life. The breed's official standard is a good place to begin this quest.

Mind and Body

Each breed recognized by the American Kennel Club is bred and judged according to an official standard established by the individual breed's national club. The standard addresses both conformation and temperament, and though no dog can live up to every element of that high ideal, it offers a guideline for what to look for when seeking a healthy, well-bred example of the breed.

The Samoyed's AKC standard is exactly what one would expect for a natural dog of such an ancient heritage as a sled dog and companion to the human species. It calls for a deep-chested, longish-legged dog built for movement, action, and stamina, a dog of good muscle and bone and a back of medium length, yet also a dog that is not quite as large as some people might expect. While its profuse coat of white hair (it must be white, cream, biscuit white, or biscuit in color) might present a vision of a rather large animal, beneath that lush growth of hair is a dog that ideally stands from 19 to 23½ inches (48–59 cm) at the shoulder and usually weighs in somewhere between 50 to 75 pounds (23–34 kg) (females are typically a bit smaller than males).

The dog's coat should be of the double variety, a soft fluffy undercoat beneath a mantle of longer, coarser guard hairs, together acting to insulate the dog from heat and cold and repelling water and snow. The dog's almond-shaped eyes should be dark in color, as should its nose, eye rims, and lips, the latter of which should also be able to curl up in what is known even in the Sammy's standard as "the Samoyed smile." The Samoyed's ears complete this attractive portrait, standing triangular and

From its dark, almond-shaped eyes to its thick coat of white hair to its lush plume of a tail carried up over its back, the Samoyed has changed very little from its days as a lifeline to the Samoyed people of the Siberian Arctic.

erect with softly rounded tips. And don't forget that signature tail, the lush plume carried up and over the back, that may hang limp on those rare occasions when the Sam is at rest.

Not surprisingly, expression, too, is addressed in the standard. In addition to a ready ability to flash its smile, you should know the Sammy by the sparkle in its eyes and its look of alert

Throughout its history, the Samoyed has charmed people with its legendary "smile," yet it is not an appropriate breed for every owner, every family.

attention. This expression should mirror its disposition, defined in the standard as "intelligent, gentle, loyal, adaptable, alert, full of action, eager to serve, friendly but conservative, not distrustful or shy, not overly aggressive." While the dog has not yet been whelped that can meet and satisfy in a single package all of these attributes, understanding the picture they combine to represent is a good start to choosing a healthy, well-adjusted Sammy pet.

Male or Female?

Another consideration when making the critical decision regarding a new pet is the question of male or female. Traditionally, in the world of dogs one assumes that the male will be more aggressive, more active, more dominant. As is typical of the sledding breeds, some Sammies may resent being housed together—particularly males with males and females with females. This can, however, usually be prevented with proper socialization during puppyhood.

Gender differences are not quite as dramatic in this breed as they are in others, with the exception of the relatively fuller ruff of fur around the neck and the larger overall size of the male. Other than that, both males and females are friendly and gregarious in their approach to the world, both relish activity, exercise, and fun, and both are equally loving toward their families and others they happen to encounter in their lives.

Adult or Puppy?

Puppies can be a nuisance; there is no doubt about that. They require a great deal of attention, guidance, and constant observation to ensure that they blossom into well-behaved, well-adjusted, healthy adults, a milestone they don't reach until they are the age of two or three years. On the other hand, there is much to be said for raising the young of a completely different species into an adult that stands as a lovely example of quintessential companion. If you do it right, you will glow with pride each time you see the light of love and respect in your dog's eyes as it gazes upon you, and accept the compliments of passersby who comment on this affectionate, well-behaved animal whom you can take with you anywhere and everywhere you go.

But don't discount the option of purchasing or adopting an older dog, either; this, too, can result in great success and satisfaction, especially with a Samoyed. Some people just don't have the time, the energy, or the inclination to raise a puppy right. An older dog—perhaps a shelter dog, rescue dog, or retired show dog—may come to you already trained and housebroken, or at least somewhat accustomed to the ways of the world. Of course, the mature dog may also come with some bad habits as well, but with the help of a qualified dog trainer or behaviorist, you can help guide the dog's behavior toward patterns that you deem more acceptable. In the meantime, take advantage of the naturally people-loving nature of this breed, and revel in the fact that this animal often exhibits a phenomenal ability to bond quickly and permanently to new owners, sometimes almost instantly.

Where to Find Your New Pet

Choosing a new pet is serious business. Once you decide that your new pet simply must be a Samoyed, you have a great deal of work ahead of you, as you must launch a quest for a companion that should remain by your side for more than a decade. Before you take the plunge, take the time to do some necessary research and explorations. There are plenty of Sams out there, most of whom would probably make fine pets. If possible, spend some time with a Samoyed or two, and of course with Sammy owners. Play with the dogs and get acquainted with their temperament and energy levels—and with the density and character of their coats. Ask as many questions as possible of the dogs' owners. Now is your chance. Before you have committed to a dog. Before you realize too late that you have made a terrible mistake.

Once convinced that you must have a Sammy of your own, the process can be tough, as nothing tugs on the heartstrings as effectively as the lovable face of the Samoyed, any Samoyed, whether it be a puppy or an adult dog. You may be inclined to go with the first Sam you meet. You may feel the urge to purchase on impulse without asking the necessary questions. Resist that urge. In the long run, it is your successful relationship with your Samoyed that will benefit from your ability to choose your new pet with your head as well as your heart.

But before you even reach that point, you must find the sources where you can meet some prospective pets. Breeders, shelters, and rescue groups are your best bets, yet all must be approached with that element of intellectual evaluation. Do that for your pet and for its breed as a whole.

The Ethical Breeder

Every once in a while, often when he or she least expects it, an individual falls in love with a particular breed of dog, and makes the momentous decision to dedicate his or her life to striving to achieve the perfection of that breed as outlined in the breed's standard. This is not, of course, the so-called "backyard breeder," the individual who decides to breed the family pet so "the kids can experience the miracle or life," or to make a few bucks off Fluffy's pups without regard to potential genetic anomalies, behavior problems, or society's pet overpopulation problem. No, we speak here of an entirely different vocation, and a vocation is truly what this is.

The ethical breeder, typically one who is breeding either for the show ring and/or, in the case of the Samoyed, the sled team, knows that there is not a lot of money to be made in this endeavor. The proper care of the mother, stud fees, puppy care, genetic certifications, and veterinary expenses can all add up. If done right and with a purity of heart, it does, often to the point where expenses surpass any money the breeder brings in from selling the puppies. The Samoyed you purchase from this individual may indeed be more expensive than that from the backyard breeder or other inferior source, but in this case, you are probably getting what you pay for.

The written contract: If you are fortunate enough to find such a breeder and choose to purchase a puppy or dog from this individual, you will probably end up with a healthy, well-socialized pet. Your peace of mind can be

An ethical breeder will sell puppies only with a detailed sales contract that addresses such issues as hereditary problems and spaying and neutering.

Whether one obtains a Samoyed puppy or an adult dog, either can blossom into a much-loved member of the family.

further bolstered by the fact that this breeder will sell every puppy with a written contract. This will include written guarantees that each puppy's parents have been certified clear of hip dysplasia and eye problems, and it will further state in writing that if at any time down the line the owner cannot keep the dog for any reason, the breeder will take it back. The ethical breeder remains responsible for each animal he or she produces for the duration of that animal's life.

Limited AKC registration: The good breeder will also include a spay/neuter clause in the contract, mandating that those puppies deemed pet quality, be altered. He or she can now also obtain what is known as limited registration from the American Kennel Club. The puppy may be registered, but because it is of pet quality, any offspring it may produce cannot be registered. This is not to say that

the pet-quality puppy is of any less value than its show-quality brethren. It simply means that it should be viewed as a pet, not as breeding stock, and for a dog, particularly for a Samoyed, there is no greater calling than that of companion. The pet-quality puppy will in turn benefit from the same diligent care and breeding as its show-quality siblings and will come with the same guarantees. But a seemingly minor fault—for instance, eyes that are a bit too light or a back that is longer than desired by the standard—means the dog should not be bred.

Finding a Breeder

To find a breeder of such dogs, ask around. Contact the Samoyed Club of America and local kennel clubs for the names of breeders in your area, and ask your veterinarian if he or she knows of any Sammy breeders nearby—perhaps a client. Another good place to meet a variety of breeders in a single location is a dog show. Check for shows in your area and plan to be there when the Sammies show. A good breeder will be pleased and willing to discuss the breed as well as his or her dogs with prospective owners at a show, but wait until after the Sammy class is complete.

Once you find some breeders, you have to be willing to ask questions.
• Does the breeder sell his or her puppies with a contract guaranteeing the health and quality of the young animals?
• Have the parents been X-rayed and deemed free of hip dysplasia by the Orthopedic Foundation for Animals?
• Have the parents been certified free of eye problems by the Canine Eye Registration Foundation?
• What does the breeder do to socialize the puppies?
• Have the puppies been inoculated?
• What have the puppies been fed to date? Is there a waiting list for puppies? (If so, be patient; the results are usually worth the wait.)
• What was it that brought this breeder to the Samoyed in the first place?

If the breeder is at all insulted or made impatient by your questions, tells you that contracts and health guarantees are unnecessary, or is anxious to sell you a puppy that is younger than seven or eight weeks of age, look elsewhere. By the same token, a breeder who is impressed by your inquiries and who grills you with questions just as relentlessly, is obviously someone who is serious about placing his or her puppies in compatible, permanent homes. This breeder is a keeper, and his or her dogs are probably keepers, too.

A Second Chance for Shelter Dogs

As we have seen, the Samoyed is not for everyone, but this does not prevent people from impulsively pur-

The interview process can be arduous but finding the right breeder and the right puppy for you is a must.

chasing a cute Sammy puppy that so resembles a stuffed polar bear toy, only to find after the animal grows a bit too large that it is too profusely coated, too headstrong, too demanding for that particular household. It is precisely such all-too-common mismatches that lead to the presence of Samoyeds in the nation's animal shelters awaiting new homes with owners who better understand their needs.

The shelter, then, is another potential source for a Samoyed pet. The staff members at a good shelter will try to learn all they can about a given dog (not always possible, of course, if the dog was a stray), and seek to match the right dog with the right adoptive owner. Knowing how the Samoyed can inspire impulsive behavior in even the most serious-minded individual, upon informing the staff of your desire to adopt a particular Samoyed, they will ask about your living situation, your daily routine, and your understanding of the breed. They should also allow you to interact with the dog (always the clincher when the prospective adoptee is a Samoyed), and of course demand that if the dog has not already been so, that it be spayed or neutered so that others of

A great deal of time and attention is required to raise puppies into well-adjusted adult dogs.

its kind will not find themselves lost, abandoned, or otherwise homeless because of too many dogs, not enough homes.

While the existence in shelters of Sammies—or any dog—is a sad testament to pet overpopulation and homelessness, the Sammy doomed to grapple with that problem is once again destined to benefit from its affectionate temperament. Unlike many other breeds, the Sam is likely to take easily and quickly to a new owner and to new surroundings. This dog was, after all, a nomad in its former native life, and it would appear that tendency remains in the dog to this day. As long as its loved ones are nearby—even loved ones it has just met—the Samoyed should live happily ever after.

Breed Rescue Opportunities

Carrying the shelter concept one step further, and ideally working hand in hand with it, is the breed rescue operation. Most breeds these days are fortunate to have within the ranks of their enthusiasts a network of dedicated individuals who work to rescue those dogs that have landed in inappropriate homes and fallen through the cracks. They care for these orphans, offer them foster care, and, if necessary, rehabilitation. They then

place them in permanent homes better suited to life with that particular breed.

While those involved in Sammy rescue cannot possibly rescue all such Samoyeds that find themselves in need of a second chance, those that are rescued have a good chance of succeeding the second time around because of the philosophy around which most breed rescues revolve. Most rely on a network of foster homes to keep the dogs in their care until they may be adopted out to their new and permanent homes. This allows the rescue volunteers to get to know the dogs and to be able to say that one can easily live in a house with cats, another adores children, another is wary of men. The more that is known about a particular dog, the better chance that dog has of being placed in a home perfectly suited to its needs. In return, those who have adopted adult Sammies from shelters and rescue groups frequently report in amazement how easily their new pets adjust to their new digs and their new families, how quickly they make themselves at home.

The adoption volunteers for a good rescue operation will be happy to chat with prospective adopters. They usually have the luxury of asking more in-depth questions than the staff at the animal shelter. For the good of the dogs they will usually stick to hard-and-fast rules, such as demanding that any Samoyed they adopt out must go to a home with a yard that has a high, secure fence and gate. Some will mandate visits by rescue volunteers to the interested adopters' home, and may even insist on meeting every member of the family and observing the entire family's interactions with the dog. While this attention to detail may border on the annoying for some adopters, it is the sign of a dedicated operation, one that probably experiences very few mismatches and returns.

Breed rescue operations are now much easier to find than they once were thanks to an increase in the public acceptance of and knowledge about their existence. You may ask for referrals from local veterinarians, breed and kennel clubs, trainers, and animal shelters, the latter of which often assist in breed rescue by notifying the appropriate groups that a dog of their breed has recently been found on the streets or dropped off by what is now a former owner. The Internet has also proven to be a boon to breed rescue. Take the Samoyed, for instance. Check into the breed's web site (listed in the Useful Addresses and Literature section in the back of this book), and you will find access to its national breed rescue, its national breed club, a very enthusiastic discussion group, and a variety of other links that celebrate Samoyeds. In the rescue pages you will find contact people, probably some in your own area, whom you can call to learn more and begin your own eligibility process. You will also find listings of dogs currently available for adoption from all over the country. Isn't technology grand?

When choosing a new Samoyed family member, spend time with your prospective pet to get a feel for its temperament and your mutual affection for each other.

Choosing the Proper Puppy (or Dog)

Just when you thought you had located the ideal source for your new Samoyed pet, you realize you have more work to do, namely, the actual choice of a new puppy or dog. Keep in mind that the words "purebred," "AKC," and "champion lines" do not automatically a healthy puppy or dog make, nor does the fact that the pup "has papers and everything." All of these elements simply mean that a puppy or dog is a purebred and is recognized as such by the American Kennel Club. The rest of the evaluation is up to the prospective owner, and a solid background in what to look for is the best way to prepare for this.

What follows are some guidelines to choosing a puppy from a breeder, yet even if you are seeking an adult dog from a breeder, shelter, or rescue group, the same considerations, to the extent that the pertinent information is known, apply to both. Learn all you can, practice what you have learned, and you should enjoy much success with your new pet for years to come.

Observe the Grounds

Upon first arriving at the breeder's facility, look around:
- Are the dogs well-groomed, well-adjusted, and healthy looking?
- Are the kennels clean and spacious enough for the occupants?
- Do the dogs seem content and relaxed in their home environment?
- Are there what you would consider too many dogs, or do you believe the population is adequate to ensure that all the dogs receive the attention, socialization, and attention they require?
- Does the breeder seem concerned about the exposure of his or her dogs to outside germs? (For example, some breeders keep chlorine bleach

Puppies whelped in a clean, loving home environment tend to be well-adjusted and thus acclimate easily to the homes of their new owners.

at the entrance to their establishments, and ask visitors to walk through a puddle of bleach solution before they get onto the grounds!)

Related to the subject of infection is that of cleanliness. In the course of your informal observations of the facility, take note of the cleanliness of the kennel area and all the necessary accessories (feeding dishes, bedding, etc.). It does not have to be as sterile as a hospital ward—it is home, after all, to rather large, profusely furred dogs—but you should be able to differentiate between, say, a normal buildup of dog hair and downright filth. A breeder that makes the effort to keep the home he or she provides for the dogs as clean as possible (and thus as healthy for the resident animals) is more likely to take similar pains in breeding and caring for those dogs. Every little clue helps.

Meeting the Puppy's Parents

Far too many puppy buyers have learned the hard way that one of the most important steps you may take in choosing a puppy is meeting the puppy's mom, and, if possible, its dad,

too. While a puppy's ultimate adult disposition is largely influenced by upbringing and environment, is it also a product of genetics and the quality of its mother's parenting skills. A shy, timid, or aggressive dam is far more likely to raise puppies in her own image because her pups spend a critical stage of their early development in her care. (By the same token, a shy, timid or aggressive sire is far more likely to pass such attributes genetically on to his offspring.) So, despite the presence of humans in the pups' environment, puppies essentially learn how to be dogs from their mother; thus, we see not only why it's a good idea to meet the mother when evaluating a litter, but also why only bitches of exemplary temperament should be bred in the first place.

Of course, the concept of meeting a puppy's parents can also apply to its "human" parents. It is just as critical to observe how the breeder handles the pups and interacts with his or her other dogs. Does the dam appear to trust the breeder? Is there a genuine respect and affection between them, or do you get the feeling the breeder simply looks at Mom and her pups as the means to a financial profit?

A good sign is a breeder who places great emphasis on temperament, one clue being boasts that these dogs are home-raised and socialized from the earliest age with children and other animals. It practically goes without saying that the Samoyed will be attractive, but the optimum pet is as classically Sammy in sweet temperament as it is in beauty. Take this very seriously and look for the dam and puppy that exemplify this goal.

Mutual Liking

Assuming that you have proceeded to this point with your head as well as your heart, have chosen a breeder with only his or her dogs' best interests in mind and who backs that up with the necessary contracts, genetic testing, and lifetime guarantees, you have now reached the moment of truth. By this point, the breeder knows whether you are looking for a show-quality puppy or one of pet quality (and the majority in the litter will be of the latter), and he or she will point you in the direction of not only the type of puppies you are seeking, but also those that seem to have temperaments that will mesh well with your own.

You must still, of course, exercise your own skills of evaluation. Watch the litter carefully and observe the interactions of the puppies. Some will be more dominant in nature; others will be more submissive. Some will be playful and inviting; others may be more reserved and aloof. Health is also critical to your evaluation. Look for the puppy with:

• bright, clear, discharge-free eyes
• healthy pink gums
• clear breathing
• clean, odorless ears
• an even, balanced gait
• skin that is free of dry patches or abrasions
• a clean anal area
• a lush, even coat.

Resist the temptation to choose a runt or a puppy that appears sickly, shy, and lethargic simply because you feel sorry for it.

Sit down among the puppies and observe their responses to you. Imagine the challenge of approaching this experience with an intellectual approach as you are tackled by a litter of adorable white fluffballs that tumble and wiggle around you and compete with each other to see just who can give you the most attention and affection. Be strong.

When all is said and done, the final choice of a puppy comes down to mutual attraction between pup and prospective owner.

Once you have spent a little time with the puppies, you will come to know their individual personalities. You will also no doubt come to understand this breed's universal love of humans, as you become the recipient of that characteristic that begins in the earliest stages of puppyhood. There will probably be one puppy that will emerge the chosen puppy; you realize you have a special liking for one another, and before you know it, that puppy has become a full-fledged member of the family. Life as you know it will never be the same.

A Samoyed in the House

Preparing Home and Family for the New Arrival

You did your homework, made smart choices, and now you are expecting the arrival of a your new Sam, but before you bring it home, it's best to prepare that home for its new and very demanding resident.

First, gather the necessities and prepare a special corner of the house for your new pup. Your Sam, for example, will need a place to sleep. It will need food, toys, grooming supplies, and food and water dishes. One trip to the pet supply store should supply you with all you need for those first days together—and beyond. Needless to say, it is best to have these in place before your Sammy crosses its new threshold. That way you can get on with the business of getting acquainted rather than running around, stressing both dog and family, as you struggle to prepare the pup's nest.

The puppy layette (and the adult dog layette, too) should include the following:
• food (both what the dog was fed before, and what you intend to feed it in the future)
• food and water dishes
• dog treats
• a nylon or leather collar of the appropriate size
• a nylon or leather leash
• grooming supplies: slicker brush, pin brush, comb, toenail clippers, pet toothbrush and toothpaste
• safe chew toys (Nylabones, lambs wool-stuffed toy, rope toy, etc.)
• bedding: blankets, towels, dog pillow
• airline crate and/or portable exercise pen
• identification tag

Security and Safety: The Benefits of Confinement

Of course, preparing for a new pet's arrival requires much more than simply purchasing the necessary supplies. The next step is getting organized, and that involves considering the benefits of confinement.

Many owners simply assume that because the Samoyed is a dog of Arctic origins, it would just naturally prefer to live outdoors. However, while Sammies as a rule do enjoy spending a great deal of time outdoors, most would like to be offered the interior of their owners' homes as their prime domiciles. Consequently, the ideal housing situation for a Sam is an indoor/outdoor arrangement.

Despite its heritage as a high-powered sled dog, the optimum living conditions for a Samoyed includes both outdoor and indoor accommodations with ample access to its family.

Living Outdoors

For its outdoor digs, the dog should have access to a spacious, secure backyard where it can lounge on the grass under a tree or romp in newly fallen snow. This yard should be enclosed within a well-constructed fence of either wood or chain link that stands at least 6 feet (1.83 m) in height and is free of gaps. The fence should be properly anchored to withstand the Samoyed's legendary digging skills, and the gate should lock with a mechanism that resists both the resident Sammy's escape attempts and a would-be pet thief. Shelter is also a concern in both winter and summer. Make sure the yard offers plenty of shelter—trees, patio awnings, deck covers, etc.—into which the dog can retreat during times of high heat, direct sun, rain, wind, and blizzard conditions. Provide the dog with a house, as well. The house should boast a leakproof roof, it should sit elevated a few inches off the ground to keep the floor dry during inclement weather, and it should be large enough for the dog to turn around in. Many styles exist, from the various traditional wood models to the new heavy-duty "igloo" houses that provide all the necessary features.

The Indoor Pet

The Sammy should also be granted liberal access to the house, where it can join in all the fun family activities that go on there. Yet, while the adult Samoyed will revel in indoor/outdoor accommodations, puppies should be housed indoors exclusively for the first few months of their lives. This is not to say, of course, that either the Sammy pup or the Sammy adult should simply be invited in and welcomed to call the entire house its home. Young or old, the dog must learn to abide by the indoor rules and respect the designated boundaries.

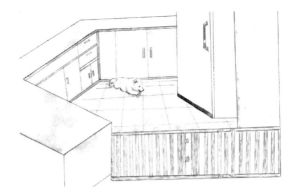

Puppies and adult dogs should have their own little corner where they can remain safely confined while their family is away.

If someone will be nearby to monitor a curious and energetic Samoyed's activities, then perhaps the dog can travel from room to room to room in its play, yet, when it cannot be watched, it must have a place it can call its own that will not only protect the home and its furnishings from a potentially destructive pup, but also extend a sense of security to the resident canine. A young puppy or even an older dog is obviously safer confined within an exercise pen in the kitchen than it would be running freely and unsupervised in the house with liberal access to such household dangers as cleaning supplies and live electrical cords.

Animal Crates

Before your new Sam comes home for the first time, decide where its little corner of the house will be, and design it accordingly. The kitchen may be a good choice, as may be the laundry room or even a corner of the family room that can be fenced off in some way. Once you have designated the appropriate area, furnish it for safety and security. An airline animal crate can provide a safe and secure home (and, as we will see, also be an

A dog crate equipped with soft bedding and enticing toys can be a comforting haven for a puppy and play an effective role in housebreaking, as well.

effective tool for housebreaking, see page 33), and indeed many an owner and many a dog swear by the crate.

To the uninitiated, a dog crate may ring more as a tool of cruel and unusual punishment than a valuable dog care tool. But when the crate is used correctly and introduced positively, the dog can learn to love it and associate it as a positive part of its home furniture. The crate can serve as a comfortable bed at naptime and bedtime, and a safe haven when the dog is feeling insecure or is left home alone for a few hours. So cast aside any hesitation about crates. Purchase one that will be large enough for the Samoyed to walk in and turn around in when it reaches adulthood. Pad it with blankets and/or towels, preferably those that carry the scent of a trusted family member, and throw in a couple of toys and perhaps a treat or two. Your pet will soon enter its crate willingly, and probably even seek it out itself in those moments of fatigue or insecurity when it just wants to rest and hide a while from the world.

A word of advice: The crate can also be abused, the dog relegated to its confines for hours and hours at a time with only brief moments of freedom to eat or relieve itself outdoors. A dog is not something you bring into your home to enjoy sporadically whenever you are struck by the whim of enjoying a few moments of canine companionship, locking it away again in its box when you tire of its antics. No, dog ownership is a full-time endeavor, and the crate must be used as a complement to your attempts to be an effective, responsible owner, not as an item to facilitate your own convenience or replace your own responsibilities.

Exercise Pens

Another confinement option is the portable exercise pen. This can offer the resident dog more room than that provided by the dog crate, and many owners may feel more comfortable with its use. Available by mail order and at pet supply stores, this collapsible structure is what you will see many dogs occupying at dog shows. Made of metal wire, it is large enough to allow the dog freedom of movement, yet compact and convenient enough to keep the animal confined in one corner of the house (or wherever you happen to travel).

As you do with dog crates, you may convince the dog to enjoy its "kennel" by furnishing it with comfortable bedding, food, toys, and perhaps a favorite dog pillow in the corner. You may even set up a crate in one section to act as the dog's bed inside its exercise pen. Set this all up in the kitchen, for example, and you have established a complete and comfortable—not to mention portable—domicile for your dog; thus you need never worry when you must leave the dog home alone for a while that you will return to find the home decimated by your pet. The dog, in turn, can relax and enjoy the knowledge of its place within the household and the family. Everybody wins.

Preventing Accidents

Legendary for its curiosity, its energy, its desire to be a part of any activity, it is not uncommon for the Samoyed to fall victim to serious, though altogether preventable, accidents. Instead of waiting for this to happen and then reliving the terrible "what ifs" after the fact, there are steps one can take to protect the Sam from its own curiosity and the danger into which that curiosity can lead it. These steps are, of course, best considered and taken before the dog enters the household.

As we have seen, this does not mean you should forbid the dog from participating in family doings or deny it access to your living quarters. Rather, those activities and those quarters should be, shall we say, Sammyproofed, in much the same way you would childproof a home. For instance, keep chemicals safely locked away, keep poisonous plants out of the home and yard, and block the dog's access to electrical cords that may appear to be tempting chew toys to the family pet (especially to teething puppies with itchy gums).

In addition to addressing everyday household dangers, consider seasonal threats, as well. While winter is the season for which the Samoyed was bred, it also holds a Pandora's box of dangers for this dog. The Samoyed is, for example, highly susceptible to antifreeze poisoning because of the many hours it typically spends outdoors in winter weather. Naturally attracted to the sweet taste and aroma of this deadly liquid, the Samoyed, unbeknownst to you, may find an open container of antifreeze in the garage, or a spilled pool of the stuff on the driveway just as you are heading

Never underestimate a young puppy's ability to seek out dangerous items in its environment. A combination of diligent environmental puppyproofing and supervision will keep the youngster safe from harm.

off to the mountains for some winter fun. Before you even realize what has happened, the dog is severely, and perhaps fatally, ill.

Even the holidays harbor dangers to this dog. The glittering glass balls on a Christmas tree can cut the mouth of an unsuspecting Sammy puppy, and a chewy Christmas light cord can cause a devastating scene. In addition, the rich food on the holiday table, if offered to the family pet, can cause a severe, and totally unnecessary bout of gastric upset (poisonous gastric upset if the food ingested is a chocolate dessert), hardly the fabric of which happy holiday memories are made.

Prevention of such scenes can be pursued by keeping the dangers out of the dog's reach, and restricting the

29

animal's access to them. In a practice instituted as soon as the dog enters its new home, the dog or puppy, when home alone, should be confined to its properly and safely appointed yard or its equally safe and entertaining corner of the house. When you are outside with your pet, simply obeying leash laws will prevent the animal from lapping up an irresistible pool of antifreeze, ingesting such items as rusty nails or broken glass, or dashing out into the street to greet a car that is unable to stop before the tires hit their white, four-legged welcome wagon. Observing these simple rules each and every day could save your dog's life. In time, they will become second nature to you.

Bringing Puppy Home

You have purchased the supplies, assembled the nest, and Sammy-proofed the house. Now what? Go pick up your new Sam, that's what. And feel confident that you are bringing it into a home that is well prepared for its arrival with a family most anxious to welcome it into its midst with open and enthusiastic arms.

It is best to bring your new pet home at the start of a weekend, a weekend where the only plan is to help the dog adjust to its new home. There will be ample time to invite friends and neighbors over to meet the new arrival so reserve the first few days for the immediate family only. This way you will help to build a strong foundation of confidence in your new pet, which may in the beginning mourn the absence of its mom, its littermates, or its foster family.

Handle your new pet gently yet firmly within those first few days. It's easy to feel sorry for the sweet thing and overpamper it in a way that actually rewards any timid or nervous feelings it may be having. By all means try to see the situation through the

newcomer's eyes, but remember, too, that it must learn to accept your family as its new pack. Remain positive and upbeat in your interactions with the dog, and help it understand from the start that it has entered a home where it is to be a very important member of the family. The Sammy, being as Sammies are, should have little trouble melding into the clan, but some adjustment is to be expected.

Nighttime

Puppies especially can have a difficult time of it, as they have been accustomed to sharing their nights amid the warmth and rhythmic breathing of Mom and their siblings. You can help convince the puppy that you are now its family by teaching it gently to accept the crate, which you may wish to place next to your own bed those first few nights so it can hear your breathing and sense that it is not alone. While many canine behavior experts don't support the idea of the pet dog sleeping in its owner's room, more owners, particularly Samoyed owners, live this way than they might be willing to admit publicly. Given the Sammy's background, this is one dog that certainly prefers this arrangement. Follow your instincts; as long as the dog knows that you are the boss and respects you as such, sleeping arrangements should cause little harm.

Diet for the Newcomer

Diet is another concern during those first few days. You may have a strong opinion about what you wish to feed your new pet, but be patient. If possible, find out what the animal was fed before it came to your house, and plan to continue to offer it that food for a few days in its new home. Even if you eventually want to switch it to some other type or brand of food, initial continuity during the first days in the dog's new home will help prevent gastric upset as it becomes accustomed to its new surroundings. Then, after a few days, you can switch it gradually over to the new food, mixing the old food with the new until the dog is being offered only the latter. The dog should of course be fed and watered out of its own dishes, which should be kept clean and placed in the same location every day so your pet will understand where it can find its rations at mealtimes.

For those first few days, keep things somewhat quiet and serene around the house. By all means play with your new pup, but allow it time alone as well to nap and to absorb all that it is experiencing. If your new pet is an older dog, take it on nice relaxing walks during the day from the very beginning to help it expend its energy and vent its stress, and to get acquainted with its new environment. Before you know it, you won't even be able to remember what the household was like before your Sam came to stay.

Establishing the Family Pack

There are few dogs as attuned to pack order and sensibility than those within the northern branch of the canine family tree. The Samoyed, being a member of this illustrious clan that evolved in teams with other dogs and life-and-death partnerships with humans, is no exception. Once you understand this fact, you earn the key to the Sammy's heart and soul.

As soon as the young Samoyed's eyes are open to the world, as soon as it realizes that there are other dogs in its midst, as well as these large two-legged creatures to whom it feels strangely drawn, it longs to know just where it stands in the hierarchy of these individuals. It is your job as this dog's caretaker to help it figure that out—and to ensure that you emerge the leader. You do this not by beating the dog into submission—a Samoyed will never stand for such treatment—but rather by ensuring that you remain consistent in your expectations of your dog's behavior, and remind the animal through your consistency that to please you, to respect you, is what it was put on this earth to do.

A Samoyed that is allowed to run wild and follow all its natural instincts unencumbered will end up a terrible discipline problem, possibly an animal-shelter casualty, a home demolition expert, and, fundamentally, a very unhappy dog. Deep down it knows that humans are meant to be its leaders, but if the humans in a Sam's life fail to accept that torch, the dog will step in and wreak havoc. It will destroy the home, chew, dig, and bark to its heart's delight, roam the neighborhood and ignore any commands to behave otherwise, and, in an extreme case, perhaps even become territorial and aggressive. To allow this to happen is unfair to the dog, to its breed, and to its species. Consequently, only those individuals up to the task of molding Samoyed behavior in a positive, consistent manner should take on the responsibility of a Sammy in the family pack.

You, in turn, must respect your Sammy by setting up situations in which it can succeed. For instance, if you bring a nine-week-old puppy into your home, you may be inclined to allow it to jump up playfully on your legs, to lounge on the furniture, and take naps on your bed. But when that puppy becomes an adult, you cannot expect it suddenly to understand that it is now too big to jump up on you and every visitor to your home, and that its coat is now too thick for the animal to be a part of the furniture. It is unfair to expect the dog to understand this. Begin to instill these subtle rules of the household when the pup is still impressionable, just as you would with a child who will someday be a teenager, and you avoid problems in communication

There are few events more exciting for a child than the arrival of a new Samoyed puppy in the family.

later on. Puppyhood is short and meant to be enjoyed, but it is also a critical time to set down the foundation of your relationship.

If you do not wish your large, well-furred Samoyed to sit on the furniture as an adult, do not allow it to do so when it is a puppy.

Establish a Routine

That foundation is also rooted in the routine you establish for your new pet and its family. Dogs are creatures of routine and feel most confident when they know what to expect from one day to the next. By establishing such a routine in the early days of your relationship, you not only foster that canine contentment, but you also convey the subtle message to your dog that, because you are the leader, you set the schedule.

The dog will be most grateful for your initiative in this area, especially because the activities around which you are building this routine are those that give it great pleasure. It will thus look to you for guidance, knowing that you will indicate when, where, and how you will be partaking of these activities. Get right on the routine, and within days the dog will understand that each day you set aside a special time for grooming, for feeding, for exercise, and, of course, for playing.

The same tenets of pack and routine establishment apply to the owner who obtains an adult Samoyed: consistency, consistency, consistency—that is the key. Establish in your own mind what you expect of the dog, enforce that daily, and bolster the bond with plenty of affection and shared activity; eventually you will see your household running like a well-oiled machine.

You will also find yourself ever amazed at the sensitivity of this dog that often seems to read the minds of those it regards as family. Children often escape discipline with a Sammy around the house for Sams do not care to see young ones scolded. Family arguments or even spirited debates are often cut short as well, when the resident Sam informs its clan in its own unique Sammy language that that will be enough of the loud voices. Invariably everyone ends up laughing and the family Sam once again stands smiling in the middle, its rich plume of a tail wagging in time to the laughter.

Housebreaking Made Easy

Housebreaking seems to be the thorn in almost every dog owner's paw, but it doesn't have to be. The problem is that so many myths abound, so many wives' tales about how to go about it, that far too many dog owners get wrapped up in that misinformation, waste valuable time, and confuse their dogs. In the time they take to practice such nonsensical methods as "rubbing the dog's nose in it" to teach the animal that it should not have defecated on the living room carpet, they could have had the dog perfectly housebroken.

Samoyeds may be stubborn at times, but deep down they truly do want to please their owners and they are not inclined to be ones to use their bathroom habits to get revenge or communicate their displeasure in an owner's behavior. To believe that the Sam, or any dog, thinks this way, is to set up all parties concerned for failure in the grand mission of housetraining.

Through Your Student's Eyes

The most productive approach to housebreaking begins by viewing the situation, and your ultimate goal, through the dog's eyes, and then arranging a training regimen at which the dog can succeed. First, most dogs will not soil their "dens," in this case their crates or beds, but most do not subsequently make the leap to including the house at large as part of their off-limits areas. Therefore, it is your job to help the dog make this leap, and it really is not as difficult and frustrating as most believe and make for themselves. You must simply dedicate yourself to responding positively to the dog, rather than resorting to the nat-

Designate an area in the yard as your pet's bathroom and whisk the animal to that spot as soon as it exhibits signs that indicate the need to do its business.

ural impulse to punish or in some other way negatively respond to the animal that does not eliminate where and when you wish it to.

First, consider the puppy, a wee being that has been on this planet for only a matter of months or even weeks. It behaves by programmed reflexes rooted in a hierarchy of dominance and submission, and spends its days seeking out fun and attention. It is not spending its time thinking, "Gee, I have to go to the bathroom. Now where should I do that?" No, when the impulse hits, it goes, giving no thought to where it is or upon what surface it is standing.

Puppies are also creatures of the moment. They require immediate

A puppy must be corrected in the act if it is to understand the lessons of housebreaking.

responses if their behavior is to be corrected in a way that they might understand. If you don't catch the pup in the act of chewing up a purse or baseball glove (which you should not have left in its reach in the first place), or in the act of eliminating on the new living room carpet, then forget it. If you scold the pup—or the older dog—hours or even minutes later, you make no progress whatsoever; the brief window of opportunity has passed. So ignore those who insist that "the dog knew what he had done two hours ago" because he crouched down with a guilty look on his face as soon as you walked in and found the books all ripped to shreds. The dog is reacting to *your* body language and facial expressions, not to what it did hours ago.

A puppy's need for immediate responses is important to keep in mind in the process of housebreaking, as are the limitations of its digestive and urinary tracts. Physically, puppies need to urinate frequently throughout the day because their bladders are quite small, and defecation is more frequent than that of adult dogs because they eat much more to fuel the energy needs of their growing bodies. Nevertheless, every day pup-

pies that are allowed to run unsupervised in their homes are punished when their owners discover calling cards left on the floor; every day puppies are having their noses rubbed in those calling cards by ignorant owners who are teaching their puppies valuable lessons in decorum. And every day such actions and the confusion they cause are impeding the progress of the training of dogs that can learn quickly and effectively if they are just taught what is expected of them.

Fast Action

Because immediacy is key to the communication required for successful housebreaking, you must keep a close eye on your pup whenever it is out and about in the house. Within a relatively short period of time, you will learn to read the signs of impending elimination: the restlessness, the sniffing of the carpet, the initial crouching. That is your signal. That is when you must act—and act fast.

As soon as you receive the signal, get the puppy outside as quickly as you can to the area that you have designated as its elimination site. (Some designate a spot indoors with newspaper as this site, but with a large outdoor-loving dog like the Samoyed, this really is not practical in the long run.) Place the puppy down on that spot, issue a command such as *"Go Potty"* (yes, you can train dogs to go on command), and when it obeys, praise the pup profusely.

Catching the puppy in the act also offers a golden opportunity. When you spot it in the act, dramatically rush over, whisk it up off the ground, and rush it outdoors to the proper place. It will finish up there in response to your commands, and again be lavished with praise. Consistency in your own fast action will help this smart little animal realize in no time just what it is supposed to do when it feels the urge.

The Owner's Role

Of course, you, the owner, have a profound responsibility here, too. Most puppies need to eliminate shortly after they eat. Because of their tiny tummies, they should be fed several times a day, so after each meal, take your puppy out to its bathroom site, issue the command, and stay out there a while until the youngster complies. Praise, praise, praise, then return to the house for a favorite game and maybe a nap.

The dog crate can be a helpful tool in this endeavor, too, because even a young puppy does not particularly wish to soil its crate. So, if the pup sleeps in its crate during the night and at naptime, for example, it will probably have to go outside when it awakens. Take it out, go through the normal routine—command, elimination, praise—and the pup is rewarded with fun and camaraderie indoors with its family until the urge strikes again.

The warning must be issued once more, however, that the crate is not to be abused. You cannot simply keep the puppy confined in its crate 24 hours a day and remove it just to eat and eliminate so that it will learn the ropes of housebreaking. That is cruel treatment of an animal that requires ample stimulation throughout the day, even at a young age. Remember: the crate is to carry a positive association, not a negative one in which the dog views it as a prison.

Should you find yourself faced with an adult Sam that is in need of housebreaking, perhaps one that was originally "trained" via the rub-the-nose-in-it method, never fear. The same techniques that are so effective for puppies will reap similar success when working with an older dog. Just remain patient, keep the dog confined when you are not there to observe it for training opportunities, act quickly, and stay alert to the signs.

Finally, if dog or puppy has an accident, the owner must accept the blame. It is his or her responsibility to watch out for the dog's needs and arrange a system in which it can learn and understand what is expected of it. In the event of an accident, then, the owner is to blame for not paying close enough attention to the telltale signs, for not communicating clearly to the animal, or for allowing the pup to run free and unsupervised inside the house. Only by correcting your own mistakes can you be an effective trainer and partner to the Samoyed in your care.

The Responsible Owner

As our society becomes more and more urban and suburban in nature, the dogs with whom we live in this ever-shrinking space are coming more and more under attack. While as a rule most owners are relatively responsible in their handling of their pets, it only takes a few in a community to cast a black mark against dog ownership. It is therefore up to each individual owner to uphold the high ideals at the core of this responsibility. Clean up after your dog (every time!), keep your dog on leash, and keep control of your pet when it is out in public.

Responsibility actually begins at home, both for the benefit of the Sam-and-owner relationship and for the benefit of society as a whole. The following are several of the issues at the heart of this responsibility that every dog owner should take seriously.

Responsible dog owners obey leash laws and make sure that their pets are always outfitted with current identification tags.

Daily romps not only help to solidify the routine on which the Samoyed thrives, but also help fortify the exquisite bond between the dog and its people.

Proper Identification

What a nightmare it is to realize that your dog, your beloved pet, is lost! You look back at the circumstances that led to this tragedy—an open door, a broken gate, a failure to obey leash laws—but that is all academic once the dog is gone. Your mission then is to find your pet, and you will increase your chances of doing so dramatically if you make the effort to identify the dog ahead of time in case the unthinkable should ever occur.

Today there are a variety of identification methods available, from high-tech microchips that are inserted under the dog's skin, to more externally visible tattoos on the groin. Each of these can be registered with agencies that keep owner information on file should the dog ever be lost, and they are excellent deterrents to pet thieves, but these are most effective when used in conjunction with what remains the oldest, most tried-and-true identification method: the collar and tag.

How simple it is for someone who finds a lost dog wandering the neighborhood, whether that be a dog-loving neighbor or an animal control officer, to take a look at the tag on the collar around the dog's neck, call the number etched there, and have the dog brought home to those who love it in no time. So keep a properly fitted traditional-buckle collar on your dog (make sure you can fit two fingers between the collar and the dog's neck), and keep those tags current. The future of your relationship with your trusted pet, or even the dog's life, could rest on that small disk of metal or plastic.

Veterinary Care

It is important for you to commit to a regimen of routine veterinary care for your pet. With regular vaccinations you contribute to broad-based efforts to keep canine illness in check, plus, attention to health will make the dog not only a better, more content pet, but an asset to the canine community as well.

Spaying and neutering are other veterinarian-based elements that enhance both dog and community. The altered Samoyed will not be contributing to the pet overpopulation problem, and it will be less inclined to be found roaming the neighborhood in search of a mate. It will probably live longer, too, which is an added bonus that cannot be ignored by those who hope to live with a particular Sam for many years to come (see The Veterinarian's Role, page 76).

Part of a young puppy's education includes trips to the veterinarian's office, where it will learn to tolerate, and perhaps even enjoy, the attentions of the doctor who will play a key role in its ongoing health and well-being.

On the Road

The Samoyed has a long tradition of travel behind it; nomadic lifestyles and polar expeditions do that for a dog. And you can carry on this tradition with your own pet. As we have learned, a Sammy is at home wherever its loved ones are, whether at the family homestead, the in-laws' house, or a mountain campsite.

Indeed, Sammies travel well, but owners must take a few steps to ensure that their pets travel safely, as well. For one thing, make sure the dog is current on its vaccinations, and bring along its vaccination records just in case you travel somewhere where such documentation could be helpful. Bring along ample stores of your dog's supplies too: food, treats, chew toys, etc. If traveling by car, institute your own canine seat belt policy, and confine your pet in its dog crate or secure it to the seat with one of the harness-style seat belts designed especially for dogs. Such efforts could save the dog's life in the event of an accident.

Also critical is your dog's identification. Make sure your pet's collar is on and stays on. Make sure the tags are in place, and keep the dog securely on leash whenever it is out and about. It is indeed a nightmare to imagine a dog being lost somewhere far from home, but it is precisely those tags that could be its one-way ticket back.

When You are Away

While traveling with your Samoyed may be your and your dog's greatest joy, the truth is, even the gentle smiling Sam is not welcome everywhere we are, and there will be times when your pup must stay at home. On these occasions, you must make arrangements to ensure the dog is well cared for while you are away.

One option is a pet sitter, but many dogs don't take well to having strangers in their homes caring for them while their owners are nowhere

A Samoyed's life will be its most rewarding if the dog is introduced to new experiences during young puppyhood.

to be seen. This is not to say that the dog will threaten or behave viciously toward the pet sitter, because Samoyeds have the reputation of welcoming strangers into the home and guiding them to the valuables rather than guarding the family domicile, but the situation may confuse the dog and cause unnecessary stress.

A better alternative may be the boarding kennel. When introduced in a positive way to canine "camp," the dog may actually view this as its own vacation. Choose the kennel carefully. Visit the facility ahead of time to make sure it is clean, that all dogs must be fully vaccinated for boarding, that the boarders are well cared for, and that the staff members know, enjoy, and love dogs. In the right kennel, which may even be at your veterinarian's office, the dog should come to know the staff (a dog like the Sam is destined to become a kennel favorite), and come to understand that, though it will be here for a while, you will return.

It is easiest to introduce the dog to boarding at a young age, which is in fact a favor you can do both for the dog and for yourself. When the day comes that you must travel without your Sam, you can leave with a clear conscience, knowing that your dog will remain content in the care of people you trust.

New Places, New Faces

Socialization to a variety of people and places is critical for any dog and an especially joyful experience for the Samoyed. Though you might assume that any special effort need not be made to accustom this gregarious animal to new experiences and people, even the Sam should receive some special attention in this area. Here are some tips:

1. Begin by introducing your new pet to as many different people as possible. The dog will adore this, and so, in most instances, will the human members of the experiment. You may then extend this to other animals, particularly to other dogs. While many Samoyeds should take readily to others of their own kind (especially when socialized vigorously to them during puppyhood), proceed with care to ensure that all the dogs involved in the introductions are amenable. This is most easily accomplished with the dogs belonging to your own friends and family members, or on daily walks in which you encounter the same people and same dogs each day. You can all get to know each other and each other's dogs—but keep a pocketful of treats handy just in case.

2. Introducing the Samoyed to new places is also a wise move. Take the dog to the park, to the lake, to the homes of dog-loving friends and relatives—everywhere and anywhere you can think of where the dog is allowed. Every effort you make in this direction not only broadens the dog's horizons and makes it a better, more well-adjusted pet, but it also stimulates and satisfies its very busy mind.

3. The Samoyed can usually coexist quite nicely with other pets, as well. But again, they must be introduced positively and with supervision. Many of the northern breeds, the Alaskan Malamute, for one, have reputations for predatory behavior toward small animals. The Samoyed is not typically mentioned in the predator group, but it can happen, so be on your guard. If you do intend to introduce your Samoyed to a pet rabbit or a young kitten, involve yourself intimately in the interaction, keep those treats on hand, and watch for signs of aggression in the dog and stress in its new prospective friend. Keep the sessions short, and in time, with continued supervision, the two should become fast friends. And if they don't? Well, that's okay, too.

4. You can count your pet's first visits to the veterinarian as important introductory experiences, as well. Upon bringing a new Samoyed, puppy or adult, into your home, a trip to the veterinarian is something that should be on the agenda early on (often a sale or adoption hinges on the veteri-

Samoyeds typically get along well with other dogs, but you can help to ensure this will be the case in its adulthood by setting up "play dates" for your young pet with other puppies.

narian's stamp of approval). As with all the new experiences to which you are introducing your new pet, keep the experience positive. Ply the pup with praise and treats, and, in keeping with its heritage, the Samoyed is likely to naturally enjoy the experience. Sure, a vaccination may be involved, but the opportunity to revel in the attentions of yet another crowd of adoring fans will make the Samoyed forget a moment's pinch at the scruff of the neck.

Training and Bonding

Understanding the Stages

Samoyeds, like every dog, go through distinct stages of development from puppyhood on. Yet many an ignorant owner out there views this dog, any dog, as simply a human in a dog suit, assuming, incorrectly of course, that the dog will just naturally view the world, reasoning and rationalizing, just as its human handlers do. The Samoyed, as intimately involved with its family as this people-loving dog becomes, is often the target of such assumptions. It seems almost human in its affection for its people, so of course it must certainly be on the same intellectual wavelength. If you allow this viewpoint to color your interactions with your pet, you may wake up one day and realize that the resident Sam has accepted leadership of the household.

Between three and fourteen weeks of age, Samoyed puppies experience the critical stage of development in which they learn to interact positively with other dogs and with humans.

The first step toward preventing this from happening and toward building a strong foundation for training is to understand the various developmental stages through which the Samoyed passes on its way to adulthood.

The Newborn

A puppy is born. Its eyes are closed; its ears are deaf to the world. Instinct guides it to the font of milk on the underside of its mother. Instinct propels its tiny body to and from the warmth of Mom and its littermates. For those first few weeks, this totally helpless predator, will do little more than suckle and sleep. Without its mother (or a surrogate human to take on Mom's duties), it will die.

At three weeks of age, the puppy reaches its first major milestone. Its eyes and ears have opened, and it is ready to begin to explore the wild world into which it has been thrust. At first this world consists solely of the whelping box and perhaps the ear of this littermate and the tail of that one. From that moment on, each day will bring new experiences to the puppy as it realizes it can interact with its siblings, it can consciously move itself from one side of the whelping box to the other, and it can even call to its mother with squeaky, high-pitched vocalizations.

The puppy has entered what many experts believe is the most critical socialization period for a young dog. This is the time from three to fourteen weeks of age, a period canine behaviorists Ian Dunbar and William Campbell refer to as the "sensitive period."

The Emerging Pup

You have heard of the age of innocence. For puppies, that critical socialization period between three to fourteen weeks should be christened the age of irresistibility. This is when puppies are at their most marketable for they emerge from the whelping box as cuddly, sprightly, delightfully interactive little creatures that wobble when they walk and charm everyone in their path.

As for the Sammy puppy, there is absolutely nothing more adorable. Consequently, disreputable types choose this as the optimum time to convince unsuspecting puppy buyers that this puppy is the perfect pet for all people in all living situations. One look at that white bear-cub face, and the targets of such a scheme simply cannot resist. Nor can they resist taking a puppy from its mother at six weeks of age, often accepted by the masses as an appropriate age, but condemned by experts as too young. Though the six-week-old pup may fare just fine away from its family, a couple of extra weeks with Mom and its siblings, for instance until it reaches seven or eight weeks of age, right smack in the middle of the "sensitive period," will give the pup just two more weeks of family socialization and littermate interactions that will have long-term effects on the adult dog's sense of contentment and security.

From a behavior standpoint, this is a time of great discovery for the puppy, and an ideal opportunity for the young animal's handlers to capture the youngster's attention. Make yourself an important figure in its life through short, fun play and grooming sessions, and convince the small animal that you have taken its mother's place. Now is also the time to begin rigorous socialization. Introduce the youngster to a variety of toys (especially chew toys, as those itchy teething gums will spur the pup on to chew on anything it

Allowing a puppy to remain with its mother until it is eight weeks old will offer the youngster the optimum opportunity to blossom into a confident, independent adult.

can find for that purpose), other (puppy-loving) dogs, and as many people as you can rope into meeting your new pet. Assuming your puppy is being protected by its vaccinations, it may enjoy a variety of experiences, all of which will add to its existence as a well-adjusted, socialized creature in the years to come.

The Samoyed tends to be slow in maturing, remaining a puppy at heart longer than some breeds do. Taking an older, more settled Samoyed as a pet may be preferable to those who love the breed but would rather not deal with the exuberant energy of a younger dog.

41

The Adolescent

The period of time between about five months of age to one year is a critical time for a young dog. It is at or around this age that many dogs, having outgrown the irresistibility of young puppyhood, are carted off to animal shelters. This is the dreaded adolescence period for a dog, and for those owners who are either unaware, unable, or simply uninterested in dealing with it in a positive, productive way, it all-too-often marks the end of the pet/owner relationship.

To imagine canine adolescence, all you need to do is think of adolescence in our own species. Scary. Yes, dogs, too, reach that stage, usually at about four, five, or six months of age, when they suddenly turn two deaf ears to the commands and requests of the owner they once clung to so unerringly. They suddenly challenge that owner, believing, just as human teenagers do, that they are now old enough and wise enough to make their own decisions. But just as we must do with their human counterparts, so must we convince the young upstart canine that no, it will not be guiding its own destiny and it will do its owner's bidding.

This does not mean that now is the time to begin beating your dog. Never! But it does mean you must steel yourself in your resolve to be consistent and to insist that the dog behave as you request. Here is where early training comes in handy, for though the mischievous adolescent may seem to have forgotten any and all commands it once knew, its selective loss of hearing and memory is but a temporary challenge. Meet that challenge by firmly putting the dog through its paces several times a day. This will jog its memory and remind the dog daily that you are still the boss.

The adolescent Sammy may appear the clown as it loses its soft puppy fluff, its legs appear too long for its body, and its ears too large for its head. It may even attempt to mask its challenges behind communicative pawing and chortling and its ever-present sense of humor. But it is soon to blossom into the swan of adulthood, and it is your job now to set a strong, well-bonded foundation that will help to ensure that you all enter the dog's adult stage with confidence and ease.

So keep that adolescent in its place, but don't try to squelch its spirit. View adolescence in a positive sense, as a necessary stage through which the dog must pass to become a well-adjusted adult. In the meantime, take advantage of its increased strength and size, and direct its adolescent energies into such activities as long walks, Frisbee training, and preliminary forays into such eventual adult pursuits as sledding, jogging, and hiking. Divert your dog's attentions sufficiently, and you may both forget that you are supposed to be grappling with canine adolescence right now.

The Adult Sam

Various breeds of dog mature at different rates, although the average age of canine maturity is considered to be about two years of age. The Samoyed, however, is an exception to the average, and defies a standard even within its own breed. While it may have matured physically by two years or shortly thereafter, its mental maturity does not usually kick in until about four years for males, three years for females. In other words, this breed remains quite puppylike in its outlook on life and the world for a very long time, a fact most enthusiasts embrace with relish, but that the uninitiated may view with annoyance.

This puppylike longevity should come as no surprise, of course, to those who have done their homework and know that this indomitable spirit demands ample family attention and the activity to match. As the dog ages, its spirit will mellow, and the bond will become even deeper as you rest upon the laurels of the history you have built together. You will look back fondly at the often manic days of the dog's young adulthood and feel privileged that you have been afforded the opportunity to share your life with such a sweet spirit.

Forging the Bond

The Samoyed thrives best under the leadership of a fair and consistent owner with strength equal to that of his or her headstrong and very intelligent—almost too intelligent—pet. The strongest bond between Sam and owner thus exists between the Sammy who has found such an owner and the owner who understands this unique need within the Sammy psyche. That bond in turn is the foundation of a successful Samoyed training program.

So how, you might ask, do you forge such a bond? Well, it is not a phenomenon that suddenly exists between the dog and the owner, nor is it a magical power with which some owners are just naturally endowed. If it were only that easy.

Building that bond takes a great deal of effort. In addition to that all-important consistency that you must practice with the pup from the very beginning of your relationship, you must also learn to respect the dog and build a system of communication upon which you can both rely. Never lose sight of the dog you are working with, a dog with intelligence and a sense of humor, with a profound allegiance to pack order and deep sensitivity to the other souls with whom it shares its home. Take some hints from this. Working with these attributes will get you much further than fighting them or attempting to change them.

Listen to your pet. The Samoyed is most anxious to make its opinions known, and it expects you, its owner, to be receptive to its messages. If you were mushing a team of Sammies across the tundra, you would certainly be wise to listen to a dog whose senses are superior to yours in detecting dangers on the ice. You can also assume here in civilization that there remains a method to the Sam's madness. So pleased will your dog be that you are listening to what it has to say that it will probably be more inclined to listen to what *you* have to say, and that is not always a given where the Samoyed is concerned.

Pack position. This will also help you earn and retain your dog's attention and strengthen your bond. Once the Samoyed knows that you are the leader, it should fall in line. This is not to say that it will become a world-class obedience champion and make your every wish its command, but it will harbor greater respect for you and be more inclined to pay attention to those commands (whether or not it deigns to obey the instant you issue a command is another story).

So, in forging this bond, revel in the give-and-take relationship you are experiencing between two intelligent beings. As you come to know each other in this special relationship, you will learn to read each other, to anticipate each other's silent signals, and receive each other's messages almost before they are sent, a phenomenon that will please the dog just as much as it pleases you. Make the effort to forge that bond, and you will no doubt come to realize just why those who have never experienced it refer to this relationship as magical, clairvoyant, remarkable. It can indeed be a thing of great beauty.

Mutual Learning

Seasoned dog trainers and behaviorists know that the key to training the dogs brought to them for lessons in manners and decorum lies not so much in training their canine students, but in training the people standing next to them. Trainers can do only so much. In an hour or two every week they can work with a dog in the class environment, but it is up to the dog's owners to carry on the lessons at home each and every day, especially during the preliminary stages of the dog's training. The trick for trainers is to figure out how to motivate their human clients to take seriously this grand mission; the trick for those human clients is to remain committed to working with the dog every day.

Another obstacle that faces the Samoyed in training is the prejudice that follows this and virtually all of the northern sled-dog breeds into the class setting. Veteran owners know that prejudice well. Broach the subject of training a Samoyed with many professional dog trainers out there, and you are likely to hear such adjectives in response as stubborn, stupid, untrainable. Obviously a trainer who would describe the dog in these terms is not someone you would like to enlist for the training of your Samoyed, nor is it someone who likely has much experience with dogs that don't happen to be Golden Retrievers or Poodles.

The Right Trainer

So, when seeking a trainer for your pet, avoid the trainer who cringes at the prospect of training a stubborn Samoyed that, in its defiance, might embarrass its trainer in front of the other students. A better choice, of course, is a trainer who understands Sammies, who enjoys their unpredictable senses of humor, and whose ego won't be bruised by a fluffy white student that would rather play a game of hide-and-seek than practice the *down* command. Also of value is the instructor who believes in working with the entire family. Such a trainer knows that the dog's eventual success in training relies on a cohesive effort from the whole family and does everything he or she can to help all succeed. Choose your trainer carefully by referrals and your own observation of his or her methods, find someone with whom family and dog alike are comfortable, and you will all reap that coveted success.

The class you ultimately choose for the proper preparation of your dog depends on the trainer, but once you find a trainer whom you are convinced will work willingly and fairly with your dog, take full advantage of the class. In other words, follow the instructor's orders, pay attention in class, and practice, practice, practice at home. You and your dog cannot learn by osmosis. You must get in there and participate.

Positive Thinking

When seeking a trainer for yourself and your Samoyed, you want someone with experience with and respect for the special world view and intelligence of the northern family of dogs. You want someone who understands the important role a dog's owner plays in the dog's training. And, of course,

Make training a game and you will have a better chance of retaining your pet Samoyed's interest in learning.

44

you want someone who truly adores dogs. But of equal importance is the trainer whose training philosophy is rooted in positive reinforcement.

In these more enlightened times, force training and training that relies on fierce punishments and negative corrections have gone the way of the dinosaurs. While some practitioners in these more archaic methods still remain, the vast majority know that there is a better and far more pleasant way. We now know that dogs, just like the people who own them, learn more quickly and more permanently when they are encouraged in a positive way to perform rather than being punished when they either refuse to comply outright, or cannot obey because they have misunderstood a confusing command. This latter event occurs all the time, often at the poor misunderstanding animal's expense.

Because dog ownership is a family affair, conscientious trainers appreciate the opportunity to evaluate their canine students' interactions with all members of their human families.

Rewards and Praise

Rewards, in the form of treats and praise offered with the immediacy commensurate with the way the dog's mind works, must be generous in such a training regimen, as should the opportunities for the dog to earn those rewards. Commands and expected responses must be communicated clearly to the dog, the instructor should take great pains to hold the dog's interest and attention, and praise and rewards should be offered as soon as the dog obeys the command.

Make Training a Game

While the Samoyed can excel in its training exercises if it feels so inclined at the moment, the repetition of training can bore this intelligent animal. The wise trainer of such a dog thus keeps the sessions short and fun, and uses his or her imagination and knowledge of the dog's personality to design training exercises that are as fun as they are educational.

For instance, if you are teaching *fetch*, try encouraging the dog to fetch a variety of objects rather than just a tennis ball over and over again. Teach the dog to play the shell game by hiding a treat in one fist and presenting both fists to the dog. Once it figures out that it is to choose, you'll practically

Even for the very friendly Samoyed, socialization with other dogs and people should begin during puppyhood, ideally in a puppy kindergarten class.

hear the wheels in its brain spinning as it looks from one fist to the other, and finally, with its paw, makes the choice. Or try using the hide-and-seek game to solidify the dog's understanding of and compliance with the *stay* and *come* commands. Have the dog stay in one room, then go and hide in another. From your hiding place, call the dog to you. Peek out and watch it look for you in every room. You'll laugh out loud at the dog's delight when it finally finds you.

Indeed, the way to a Samoyed's heart is through fun and games. Keep this in mind, keep it positive, and you'll be amazed at how quickly and effectively this dog with a reputation for stubbornness and "stupidity" learns not only the basic commands, but the rules and guidelines of a great many organized games and activities as well.

Puppy Kindergarten

It used to be an accepted axiom that a dog could not begin its training until it reached the arbitrarily chosen age of six months. That has now changed. All we need to do is observe the mother dog to figure out that training can begin right away. Mom does this with her young, and we can and should do the same once the puppies are turned over to us.

Validating the idea that a very young puppy is perfectly capable of learning the basic commands is the puppy kindergarten class, a formal class offered now in most communities in which young puppies congregate with their owners and a so-called "kindergarten teacher" to learn the basic commands. Most of these classes mandate that the students be at least three months of age (the pups could learn earlier, but this ensures that all have had the majority of their puppy vaccinations by the time they come to class), and the techniques used are designed to appeal to their infantile sensibilities.

While young puppies are avid students, they will only remain so if they perceive school as a game. The trainer and the owners with whom he or she is working must pull out all the stops in attracting and retaining the puppies' attention. The messages of what is expected of them must also be broadcast clearly, and the resulting treat rewards must come fast and furiously.

The kindergarten class usually begins with a play session, in which all the puppies can play and wrestle together. This not only helps them to expend any excess energy they may be harboring that might hinder the subsequent class, but it also serves as a valuable socialization experience. The pups learn to enjoy and play with a variety of other pups of all shapes, sizes, and colors, and it is indeed a wonderful sight to behold.

Once the play session is complete, training begins. Within days—and with the help of treats and games—these young students are sitting on command, fetching favorite toys, and even coming when their owners call them. Indeed, when trained with the proper attitude, the puppy will view the *come* command as especially joyful, for it learns that when the owner calls to the puppy with such enthusiasm, the pup knows that if it obeys it will be amply rewarded. It is critical that beyond class the owners continue to work each day with their youngsters in short sessions scattered throughout the day. This benefits not only the puppy's permanent learning of the basic commands, but also the building of a foundation between the pup and its owner, setting the course for the partnership and the more in-depth training that lies ahead.

Fostering Obedience

Veteran Sammy owners, breeders, trainers, and the like never hesitate to recommend that every Samoyed attend formal obedience classes, preferably a series of them. While ideally this is true for every dog, the northern dogs and the people who love them draw particular benefit from heeding this advice. As we have seen, the Samoyed and its cousins, sprung from a dangerous land where often their brains as well as their brawn were necessary to keep them alive, can in modern times march to the tune of their own drummers. They may remain loving and affectionate to their owners, but when it comes to their behavior, if given their heads, they will act independently from what might be desired by those they call family.

This is not to say that your goal should be to take your Sam to a national obedience championship. If that is your personal goal, then by all means pursue it, but don't be disappointed if your pet has other ideas. Samoyed obedience champions are few and far between, not because they don't have the brains to master the skills involved, but because they have too many brains to obey their handler's every command in a situation that they may deem has little purpose. Harness them to a sled, on the other hand, and ask them to turn left or right, and in unison they will obey, assuming, of course, you are not asking them to run into an unseen crevasse in the ice ahead, in which case, you are wise to obey the dogs.

So, though your Samoyed may not be earning medals and multiple titles in the obedience ring, obedience training is nevertheless of great value to this dog. While it helps the dog learn the basic commands, that is almost secondary to the value of this training to your fundamental relationship. As you work together, you learn to communicate with your pet with simple verbal commands and hand signals, and the dog learns to read those signals. You then emerge as a bonded pair, able to bridge the communication gap between your two diverse species.

Obedience training also helps to remind the dog in a gentle way that you are the boss, and that is of profound benefit to this animal. What the dog will not realize from its training exercises is that in learning its manners it is opening doors for itself in the future. A well-behaved dog that can be controlled by its owner in public situations is much more likely to be invited along on camping trips, shopping excursions, and afternoon picnics in the park. The Samoyed that knows how to behave will be as welcome in those venues as it is beautiful—and provide excellent PR for its species at the same time.

The Necessary Equipment for Training

When we embark on the grand mission of dog training, we imagine in our minds the end product of a perfectly trained dog, obeying each command without question, without fail—and all performed without benefit of a leash. But this image really is not realistic for most people, or for most dogs, due in part to the leash laws enforced in most communities. This does not mean you should give up on your dream, however; just proceed with the proper equipment.

Types of Collars

All dogs should wear a collar at all times, even lushly coated Samoyeds whose collars may interrupt the lovely line of the thick ruffs about their necks. The collar, complete with current identification and license tags, is not only a necessary canine wardrobe item, but can also be a valuable training aid.

First, there is the traditional buckle collar, a simple accessory for walking the dog on leash. For training, however, many trainers and owners prefer the chain, or choke, collar. This is a

A properly fitting collar is one of the most important pieces of equipment in dog care. This applies to both the leather or nylon collar the dog wears at all times and the chain collar it wears for training.

chain with two large rings on each end. The chain threads through one of the rings, creating a nooselike loop that fits over the dog's head. The leash then attaches to the other ring. When the handler tugs on the leash, the collar tightens around the dog's neck, ideally as a signal to the animal that it has responded incorrectly to a command or other signal from the handler.

Used incorrectly, chain collars can be painful to a dog, and today more

There is a right way and a wrong way to place a chain training collar on a dog. Assuming that the dog will be walking on its handler's left side, the dog on the left is wearing the collar correctly. The dog on the right is wearing it incorrectly.

and more trainers are beginning to criticize their use, claiming that even when used correctly they can harm the neck. An additional problem is that chain collars are also often placed incorrectly on dogs by well-meaning owners. There is a right way and a wrong way to put the collar on the dog. To place the chain collar on the dog the right way, imagine facing the dog with the looped collar in hand. The collar should mimic the shape of a backward "6" as you place the loop over the dog's head. Now, assuming the dog is walking on its owner's left side as is classically done, the correctly placed chain collar should loosen automatically as soon as pressure is released from the leash. Incorrectly placed, however, it will stick.

Warning: The chain collar should never be used as the dog's regular, everyday collar as it may catch and fatally choke the dog.

Unfortunately, seen far too commonly these days are the so-called prong or pinch collars. These are metal collars with blunt metal studs that dig into the dog's neck when the leash is pulled. Needless to say, these collars are frequently misused, the dogs that are wearing them needlessly abused. While there may perhaps be a minute minority of dogs that can benefit from this type of collar (as long as the owner is well trained in its use by a qualified instructor), a Samoyed is not one of these. People seeking shortcuts and get-trained-fast gimmicks probably should not own a dog in the first place, and far too often it is these people who employ pinch collars in their quest to make training as quick as possible on dogs who have no business even being in the same room as one of these collars.

Harnesses

Another collar option isn't really a collar at all, but an H-shaped harness.

While some Samoyed owners claim that the feel of the harness seems to touch the ancient sledding instincts in the dog that make it want to pull ahead, others have found it helps keep their dogs under control, perhaps by imparting a sense of security to the dog that it misses from a collar simply wrapped around its neck. The harness is no doubt more comfortable for the dog, and it can give owners an increased sense of control, as well.

Halters

Another recent development in canine equipment is the halter, which fits over the dog's muzzle and resembles a halter worn by a horse. Dogs wearing halters still receive double takes from passersby not accustomed to seeing dogs so outfitted, but they are becoming more popular and are quite effective and humane in their effects on the dogs that wear them. Halters can, however, be misused, and the owner is best trained first by a trainer skilled in their use.

Rx for Potential Problems

Every year dogs are sent to the nation's animal shelters because of behavior problems. On the surface, this seems simple enough, but delve below that surface and you will find a situation much more complicated than it seems.

First of all, most so-called behavior problems are simply natural canine behaviors that owners are incapable of directing in more positive directions. Chewing, for example, is not only a natural response to a young teething dog's itchy gums, but is also an effective stress-relieving response in adult dogs. It is unfair, even downright cruel, to expect a dog not to chew. The behavior can be facilitated positively by supplying the dog with acceptable chew toys that it can use in lieu of furniture, books, or other

Although your dog may appear to exhibit remorse while being scolded for a misdeed, it is actually reacting to your angry voice and body language. A dog must be corrected in the act if it is to understand that it has misbehaved.

valuables that are not designated for canine chewing impulses.

Far too many owners, however, find it easier just to dump the dog than to explore the cause of its behavior and work to correct it. What these individuals may also not realize is that there is help available in the form of qualified animal behaviorists. A behaviorist is not necessarily the same as a trainer, the former being a specialist in dealing

Chewing is a natural canine behavior for both puppies and adult dogs. Offer your pet safe chew toys of its own so that it will not seek out and destroy the possessions of other family members.

with natural canine behaviors and problems rather than simply training a dog to obey certain commands. A skilled behaviorist can in most cases come in, diagnose the situation, and prescribe a remedy program the owners may institute to get everyone back on the straight and narrow.

Certain dangerous behavior problems—aggression and biting, to name two—should most definitely be addressed by a behaviorist, who may in turn be able to rehabilitate the dog or determine that euthanasia is the only answer. But most everyday complaints can usually be addressed by the owners themselves. Slow to mature as it is, the Samoyed may partake of these behaviors longer than most, so understanding their genesis is of special value to Sammy owners. The following are the big three of this category, natural behaviors that need not be squelched altogether or allowed to run wild, but that can be corrected for the contentment of all parties concerned.

Chewing

All dogs chew. Puppies are the most enthusiastic participants in the activity given the emergence of teeth that causes mouth discomfort requiring chewing for relief. But older dogs chew, too, often because chewing is an excellent outlet for stress relief. All too often, when a dog chews a valued possession of its owner, the owner neglects to acknowledge that perhaps he or she should not have allowed the dog to run loose unattended and unsupervised through the house while the owner was away, or left valuable items out within the dog's reach. Instead, the dog bears the wrath, usually long after it has done the deed and was able to equate the owner's anger with its own actions. The result: angry owner, confused dog, a no-win situation.

The remedy to this is simple: Keep your pet confined when you cannot monitor its actions, and supply the dog with its own attractive and safe chew toys so it will not seek out the possessions of its owner. Chew toys are available in every size, shape, color, and texture, and every dog has its preferences. In time you will learn what your dog prefers. Listen to what it tells you and you need never have to deal with chewing as a "behavior" problem.

Digging

If you spot a dog digging just once, you will understand instantly just why this is such an attractive habit. Rarely will you see a dog in such ecstasy, flinging dirt, vegetation, mud, whatever lies in its path, skyward with tornado-like paws, reveling in the release of energy, gloating over its accomplishment when it reviews what it has done. With centuries behind them of digging in snow to create sleeping spots and whelping areas, dogs of Arctic breeding are especially adept at this skill, able to transform a backyard into a maze of trenches of battlefield proportions in the blink of an eye.

Given the great joy and release digging offers a dog, it would be a shame to deny it this outlet altogether, but neither can most people afford to allow the landscaping to be demolished on a regular basis. The remedy is in the compromise. If your dog loves to dig, as most Sams do, set aside a corner of the yard as its digging spot. Teach it that here and only here is where digging is allowed by burying a favorite toy or bone in the spot and encouraging the dog to find it. Praise the dog for excavating in that spot, and fence off particularly sensitive areas of the yard such as the vegetable or rose garden. If you don't have a yard, take the dog to the beach or some other sand or dirt-rich area for an occasional dig, prepare for a thorough grooming afterward, and you'll all live happily ever after.

Barking

Samoyeds may not be watchdogs in the classic sense. Would-be thieves don't necessarily know that, however, and it's a safe bet that the dog's love of barking has deterred many a potential break-in. While this is one benefit of barking, the downside is a dog that barks too much, driving its owners and everyone within earshot crazy.

Incessant barking is often caused by separation anxiety or boredom, either of which may be remedied by ensuring that the dog receives ample exercise and attention from its owners every day to help it expend that excess, bark-producing energy. As for barking simply for the love of barking, this may be channeled by teaching the dog that if it hears a sound, yes, it may bark to inform you of it, but then it must quiet down. Praise the dog for the initial bark, call it to you, have it sit or lie down by your side, and praise it again. In time the dog should learn that barking to a point is allowed. Barking simply for the joy of hearing oneself bark, however, is not.

Basic Training

There is no one true and proper way to train dogs, although most in the field hold to specific techniques and philosophies that their experiences have led them to believe are the most effective. Indeed, ask ten different professional trainers for their opinions on how to train a dog to *heel,* for example, and you will receive ten different dissertations on this fine art. Some recommend treats; others abhor their use. Some use training collars; others prefer the regular collar, and still others now swear by the halter. As long as the various methods are rooted in positive reinforcement and a commitment to seeing the world through the dog's eyes, they are on the right track.

The following "How-To" section offers some basic instructions for one way to train dogs in the basics with verbal commands, and in some cases hand signals too (it's handy for a dog to learn hand signals when it is young, so that someday, as a senior citizen that may have lost its hearing, it will still understand its owner's commands). This is not of course the only way, or even the way that your dog might take to most readily. But it is a start.

So gather some treats and snap on the leash and get started. Remember, though, that dogs of the Sammy's intelligence tire quickly of the repetition of training and will shut down completely when handled with anger or impatience. Keep the lessons short and interesting and the mood light and positive; end each session by insisting the dog obey the final command, and you will discover the formula for success.

Common Training Mistakes

One major error many owners make in using the *come* command is to punish the dog for obeying. How many times have you seen a dog turn a deaf ear to its owner's request that it come? The dog finally concedes, creeping sheepishly, hesitantly, toward the now-hysterical owner, only to be punished verbally and/or physically for complying. What kind of message is that sending to the dog?

The more effective, not to mention logical, method of retrieving a wayward off-leash dog is to maintain a positive attitude, even if this dog that you raised from puppyhood is pretending it has never seen you before in its life. Call it to you exuberantly. Once it arrives in your arms, resist the temptation to scold it for taking so long to get there, and praise it for finally complying. That way the dog builds trust in you, it knows that it will be rewarded not punished, even when it has not responded as quickly as you both know it should, and it will be more likely to come to you willingly the next time.

HOW-TO:
The Basic Commands

The down *command comes in handy when you need to help an overly exuberant Sammy settle down.*

Sit

The *sit* is the most basic command, and the one that dogs learn most readily because it is a position that they naturally take themselves even when not being commanded to do so. While some trainers may suggest teaching this command by pulling back on the leash or pushing down on the dog's rear end to let it know it is to sit, it is usually more effective not to touch the dog during the command phase of training so that the animal might believe that obeying is its own idea.

An easier, non-touch method is to hold a treat in your fingers and hold your hand over your standing dog's head. It will catch the scent of the treat, plus be curious as to why your hand is

In a simple method to teach a dog the sit *command, hold a treat up above the dog's head and move it back toward its tail. As the dog follows the treat, it will end up sitting.*

there, and will automatically look up. When it does, move your hand slowly back in the direction of the dog's tail, all the while issuing the command *"Sit."* Before the dog even realizes what has happened, it is sitting down, at which point it should also be rewarded with the coveted treat and words of praise. So pleased will it be with its performance that it will probably pop right up again and wiggle around in delight, offering you another opportunity to teach this command.

As the dog becomes better skilled in this, you can embellish your command with the commensurate hand signal. One suggestion is to draw an invisible "J" in the air as you issue the *sit* command. In time the dog should learn to obey the hand signal alone without benefit of an accompanying voice command.

Down

A technique similar to what you used for the *sit* can be used to teach the *down*—and in a natural progression. Command the dog to sit, and then, with that trusty treat again within your fingertips, hold the morsel at the dog's nose and slowly move it down in a straight vertical direction as you issue the *down* command. The dog will follow the treat down with its head and its front legs until, voilà, it is lying down. Praise and a treat are in order for the pup.

For the accompanying hand signal, hold a flat hand out toward the dog, your palm facing the ground. Lower the hand with one smooth motion toward the ground as you say the magic word. Whether issued by voice or hand signal, the *down* command comes in handy when an overly exuberant Sammy is getting a bit carried away in its greeting of guests to its home. The Sam that will lie down in the midst of its revelry will have an opportunity to settle down while it is in its prone position, after which it may resume its greeting but in a somewhat more subdued fashion.

Heel

This is one command that you may have a bit of difficulty teaching to a Samoyed, a dog that was bred to lead and to pull, not to follow politely along either beside or behind its owner. Nevertheless, if you intend to compete in obedience with your pet, heeling is a skill it must learn. Again, treats can help as you walk forward, the leashed dog to your left, your goal to convince the dog to remain at your heel as you walk, the leash draped loosely in the shape of a "J."

It may take a while for your dog to conquer its genetic predisposition to pull, but be patient. If, on the other hand, you do not intend to seek glory for your Sam in the obedience show ring, it is probably enough simply to teach your dog to walk without pulling on the leash and forging ahead, which actually better facilitates the dog's natural desire to explore all those wonderful scents and surprises it encounters in its path on a daily walk. The dog need not walk at the perfect *heel*, but it should learn to walk beside you without pulling your arm out of the socket.

One way to get this message of walking decorum across is to walk straight ahead with the dog on leash, and then, without warning, make an abrupt about-face and head off in the opposite direction. The startled dog will follow. Do this several times over the course of as many days, and soon the dog will realize that perhaps it should pay a bit more attention to what you are doing and where you are going.

Stay

Handy whenever you want your dog to remain in place, the *stay* command is best taught from the beginning with a hand signal, which demonstrates to the animal exactly what you want it to do. To begin, place the

When teaching your dog the stay *command in an open public area, keep the animal on a long leash to prevent mishaps.*

dog in a *sit,* then issue the *stay* command and begin to back away (if you are in an unenclosed public area, keep the dog on a long lead to prevent it from bolting). At the same time, hold your hand out toward the dog, open in a *stop* position, the hand held perpendicular to the ground, the open palm to the dog. Walk back only a few steps, then return to the dog and praise it profusely for staying in place.

The smart Sammy will figure this one out in no time, and practice of the stay command will become a game as you increase the distance you move away each time. The plot and the fun then thicken when the next command is introduced to the mix.

Come

One of the most important commands for a dog to learn—and one of the most challenging for it to obey—the *come* command can literally save a dog's life should it agree to obey in the face of an oncoming car or other pending danger. But not all dogs feel inclined to obey, especially when a particularly fascinating

scent is beckoning from behind a faraway tree or a friendly looking dog is waiting to play at the other side of the park. Nevertheless, it is an important command to teach, and to keep teaching, throughout the dog's life.

For ease and efficiency, teach the *come* command in conjunction with the *stay* command. Teach the stay first, and once the dog has that one somewhat down, add the *come*.

Place the dog in a *sit-stay*, issue your *stay* hand signal and command (here, too, employ a long lead if the lesson is being held out in the wide open spaces). Move backward. When you are several steps away, call the dog to you in a happy, joyful voice. Flash a treat if you like, and beckon the dog toward you with your hand. You might issue a simple *come* command, but the dog may get the idea more quickly if you offer invitations that it will be simply unable to resist. The dog comes, is rewarded, and can't wait to do it again, this time with a longer distance between the two of you before you invite it to come forward.

The Well-Nourished Samoyed

Dogs Living Longer

Dogs are living longer today than dogs of any previous age. A combination of factors account for this, including a more acute awareness of potential health problems on the part of breeders, and major advancements in veterinary medicine.

However, an equally stunning factor is found in the improvements made in canine nutrition in the past two or three decades. This trend is evident not only in the fact that the subject is enjoying increasingly serious treatment in veterinary schools, but also in the increase of pet owner understanding of the impact nutrition has on dogs' overall health. This is vital knowledge, for nutrition offers the dog owner the power to contribute to the quality and longevity of his or her pet's life as never before.

To wield this power, however, is a personal choice. If the owner chooses to ignore this golden opportunity, to supply the dog with an inadequate diet, supplemented with inappropriate treats and table scraps, instead of adhering to the sound, quality diet that facilitates canine health, the dog will miss the great benefits that well-balanced nutrition can provide.

Historically, the Samoyed trusted the Arctic people with whom it lived and worked to share their food with the dogs that were their lifelines. Today's Samoyeds look to their more contemporary owners, trusting that they, too, will provide them with what they need to work, to play, and to enjoy life to the fullest. To fall down on this responsibility and allow the Samoyed, a dog with a very rich and athletic past, to become obese and follow an inactive lifestyle, is an insult to the breed's heritage. By the same token, to learn all one can about the optimum canine diet and to commit to offering this to one's Samoyed pet, is a tribute both to the breed and to the advancements that have made enrichment of the dog's life possible.

Canine Nutrition Basics

The first step toward providing the Samoyed with the diet it needs for optimum health is to understand the components—the building blocks—of canine nutrition. These include proteins, fats, vitamins, minerals, and carbohydrates, all of which must not only be present in the dog's diet, but present in the correct quantities and balances that will foster the overall functioning of the dog's system. In a complex waltz of chemical wizardry, the nutrients must be combined in just the right configurations to ensure the dog will be neither overnourished nor undernourished. Indeed, where nutrition is concerned, if a little is good, more is not necessarily better—and, in fact, it can be downright dangerous.

Proteins

Bones, muscle, and blood, to name only a few of the body's vital tissues, require a constant supply of high-quality, easily accessible, digestible protein to keep them in top form. Because dogs, like humans, are more omnivorous than they are pure carnivores, meaning that the healthy canine diet includes both animal and plant material, this protein may be derived from both animal or plant sources.

That dogs require protein is certainly no stunning newsflash, but what many dog owners do not realize is that the protein needs of a puppy, for example, are far greater than those of a canine senior citizen. Despite such differences, however, the need for the highest quality protein is standard for all dogs, young and old, couch potato and athlete alike.

Carbohydrates

Imagine the energy required for the healthy Samoyed to wag vigorously that large plumed tail that curls up over its back. While tail wagging may seem to be no more than a simple canine reflex that we tend to take for granted, such action requires energy. Much of that energy comes from carbohydrates, which typically come in turn from grains common in commercial dog foods, such as corn and rice. Obviously, then, a canine diet consisting of nothing but raw meat simply would not satisfy the variety of nutrients a dog requires from its food.

Fats

While obesity can be a serious problem for dogs, the fact remains that, along with carbohydrates, fat is a nutrient essential to fueling the dog's energy needs. These needs, of course, will vary from dog to dog depending on age and activity. A four-year-old Samoyed that leads a sled dog team, for example, will require far more fat in its diet than will a 12-year-old retired show dog whose daily exercise routine consists of strolling along a Florida beach with its owners. Fats, which, like proteins, may be derived from either plant or animal sources, are higher in energy than are carbohydrates, but if the dog's energy needs exceed the energizing nutrients in its diet, malnutrition will result. If the reverse is true, you will end up with an overweight, and very unhappy, Sammy.

Vitamins and Minerals

Vitamins and minerals play critical roles in virtually every function of the canine system, yet they also provide the fodder for the most prevalent forms of nutritional abuses. Dietary supplements abound on the market, accompanied by emotional testimonials on how this vitamin or that mineral corrected a particular dog's health problems, or even saved its life. But most experts agree that if a dog is offered a high-quality, "complete and balanced" commercial diet appropriate to its age and circumstance, it does not need such supplements, which in some instances may actually prove to be detrimental.

Fat-soluble vitamins—vitamins A and D, for example—unlike the water-soluble Bs and C, can accumulate in the dog's body and ultimately cause problems, such as weight loss and kidney damage. The same is true of minerals, many of which must be in balance with each other to do their jobs properly. For example, a deficiency or oversupplementation of calcium, a mineral critical to bone growth, will throw phosphorus off kilter, and the two must be balanced to perform their duties properly. So, unless an owner is a highly trained canine nutritionist, he or she is wise to leave the diet formulations to the experts.

Water

In the midst of the chemistry and alphabet soup that is canine nutrition, we may overlook another important component of the dog's diet—perhaps the simplest: water. Water is the mortar that binds all the other nutrients

A high-quality diet will help to keep a Samoyed healthy internally, which will be exhibited externally in the dog's conformational structure, bright-eyed expression, and healthy skin and coat.

nutrition, and they have emerged quite successful in this mission. The diets they have designed, generally formulated by veterinarians and animal scientists who are the reigning experts in the field, are readily available at grocery stores, feed stores, pet supply stores, and veterinary offices. Most dog owners can thus feel fairly confident when purchasing a high-quality brand name commercial dog food that the diet they choose will meet their pets' nutritional needs.

But how can you be sure? By reading the labels, that's how. This can be a bit confusing, however, unless you know what to look for. Simply reading the words "chicken" or "beef" on a label does not mean that the chicken or beef in that can or in that bag are of the high quality necessary for effective metabolism. The higher the quality, the more accessible the nutrients to the dog's system.

Unfortunately, on their surface, dog food labels don't help you to gauge the quality of the ingredients, so, with hundreds of brands of dog food on the market today, you must learn to read between the lines.

By law, dog food packaging labels must present:
• a guaranteed analysis of the crude protein, crude fat, crude fiber, and moisture content of the food
• the name of the species the food is intended to feed
• a listing of ingredients in descending order of content
• a nutritional statement, such as "complete and balanced for all life stages" or "complete and balanced for growth," etc.

But what is far more significant in terms of quality is the package that also displays a statement about Association of American Feed Control Officials protocols.

The AAFCO sets minimum and maximum nutritional guidelines for pet

and their functions together, facilitating digestion and absorption, assisting in cell function and health in every tissue of the body, and maintaining an efficient circulatory system.

Winter or summer, dogs must have access to fresh, clean—and in the summer, cool—water at all times. This can be a bit of a challenge during winter for the snow-loving, athletically inclined Samoyed, which, like many other northern breeds, may not be interested in lapping up the wet stuff on a subzero morning before embarking on a rousing sled journey. Veteran mushers meet this challenge by spiking the water with meat broth or some other favored flavoring, transforming the water into a delicious nectar no self-respecting Sammy could refuse.

Deciphering the Labels

Pet food companies have spent a great deal of time, money, and effort to uncover the secret of balanced canine foods. A food that meets those standards, ideally through the test feeding of dogs, will indicate that on its package. The manufacturers of most high-quality foods are proud to state that their foods have been tested successfully in this way, just as they are equally pleased to answer consumer questions about quality, ingredients, food choices, and feeding strategies via their toll-free question lines. The pet food industry is a big, competitive business. Take advantage of this, and use the resources available to learn as much as possible about the food you choose to feed your trusted pet.

Proper nutrition is a key ingredient in helping your dog to remain healthy and spry for many years to come.

Choosing the Right Diet

A variety of considerations come into play when choosing the ideal diet for your dog. We humans may pity our pets for the lack of variety in their diets, but they will remain far healthier consuming one high-quality food than they will joining the family for a four-course gourmet meal, or receiving a different brand or flavor every other week. Such frequent changes can cause digestive upset as well as foster a finicky palate.

Dog foods are packaged in several forms, the most common being dry food in bags and moist food in cans. Also available are semimoist foods packaged in burgerlike cakes or soft tidbits, but these tend to contain more additives and colorings, and they don't always agree with every dog's digestive system.

The cleanest and easiest food to feed, of course, is the dry food that, assuming it is of the "complete and balanced" variety, will sustain a dog just fine as its sole diet. The canned varieties, as meaty as they are, offer a bit more flavor, yet they are messier to feed, especially when the dog leaves food in its dish after mealtime. The feces canned foods produce are also softer and more difficult to clean up

than those from a dog on an exclusively dry diet.

While some owners prefer feeding their dogs dry food exclusively because of its convenience and lack of odor, others take advantage of both

The ins and outs of canine nutrition can be a bit confusing, but adhering to common-sense guidelines in the management of your pet's diet will make a profound contribution to the animal's health, longevity, and well-being.

Commercial dog foods come in dry, canned, and semimoist forms, and in an endless variety of flavors.

options and mix a little canned food into the dry for flavor. In addition to cleanliness and convenience, an added benefit of dry dog food, with or without canned supplementation, is the positive effect it has on a dog's teeth. While a dry diet cannot replace the need for routine dental cleanings by a veterinarian, hard, dry foods can help keep the teeth clean between professional cleanings.

Dog foods today are produced with a variety of ingredients, as well, combinations of such meats as beef, chicken, and lamb, with such grains as corn, rice, and barley. As a result, flavors vary, and most dogs do have their preferences, or are able to digest some ingredients more easily than others.

Many a breeder of Arctic dogs also suggest that these dogs be fed a bit of fish every week or so, in keeping with the diet they were fed, in the Samoyed's case, for thousands of years in the Arctic. It appears that some commercial pet food manufacturers are now also heeding this message that on its surface may sound like breeder folklore, and are now

including fish and fish oils in their commercially produced foods.

Regardless of what type of food you ultimately choose for your pet, when a new dog or puppy first comes into your home, continue to feed the animal whatever it was fed previously. If you do switch it to a different food, do so gradually, mixing the old with the new over a period of several days, until the dog is eating only the new food and has been spared any digestive upset a sudden change can cause.

Special Diets for Special Needs

While the choices and quality of dog foods have skyrocketed in the last few decades, so has the number of specialty foods formulated for dogs with special needs. Matching these foods to the dogs that need them can help to promote good canine health and perhaps enhance the animals' enjoyment of life.

Low-calorie Diets

Far too many dogs these days are fed far too much, the excess typically comprised of table scraps and an overabundance of treats. Combine this with a lack of sufficient exercise, and the result is a dog with a weight problem.

To determine whether your dog falls into this category, conduct this simple test: Dig your fingers into your Samoyed's deep white coat, and run them down the dog's rib cage. If you cannot feel the ribs, it's time for a diet. If you feel the ribs too distinctly, too sharply, and you detect no surrounding tissue, that dog needs a bit more meat on its bones. Ideally, you should be able to feel the contours of each rib, but you should also feel the surrounding tissue, indicating that the dog is lean yet healthy, in other words, just right.

Without benefit of the rib test, it is often difficult to determine just what shape a Samoyed is in under all that thick white hair. While one is less likely to see an overweight Samoyed than some other breeds more prone to obesity, fat Sammies are out there and they are sad sights to see. When such a dog is pronounced by a veterinarian to be overweight, a condition that will shave years off its life and contribute to a variety of related health problems, the dog needs to cut down on the fat and calories, but it need not feel deprived. Today, overweight dogs are fortunate to have access to foods specially formulated to be low in calories and fat, but high in volume and flavor. In most cases, the major challenge is to convince the dog's owner to change his or her habits, to learn to say no to the dog's insistent pleadings for inappropriate and/or excessive food and treats.

Puppy Diets

The healthy Samoyed can put on 40 to 50 pounds (18–23 kg) during its first year of life. Needless to say, it must thus be offered a complete and balanced diet high in energy and all the quality ingredients it will require to fuel that rapid growth. This can be easily supplied with one of the fine puppy foods currently on the market.

The puppy, because of its active metabolism and small stomach, will need to eat several times a day, but if you feed it too much, the overnutrition may actually hinder optimum growth and lead to health problems. Following the manufacturer's, breeder's, and veterinarian's guidelines on feeding schedules and quantities for the first 12 to 18 months of the puppy's life can help lay the foundation for both good health and healthy eating habits in the years to come.

Geriatric Diets

Just as puppies come into the world with special dietary needs, so may older dogs require some special considerations, as well. As a dog ages, its activity levels may wane, as will its need for high-energy foods. As we have seen, too many calories combined with a lack of activity will make for an overweight dog. This can be dangerous for an older pet that may already be experiencing the onset of an age-related slowdown of the internal organs. Although the need for geriatric diets is still a subject of debate (unless the dog is overweight), there are foods available that offer a canine senior citizen fewer calories, less fat, easier digestibility and a reduction of sodium and protein. Discuss the need for these foods with your veterinarian.

High-energy Diets

While most pet dogs who participate in some type of moderate athletic activity each day will fare well on a so-called "maintenance" diet, some dogs—for instance, a team of racing sled dogs or a Sammy that regularly accompanies its owner on long-distance runs—may require a food higher in energy than is offered by a regular maintenance diet. On the other hand, feeding such a diet to a pet Sammy with average activity levels can lead to obesity and the problems associated with overnutrition.

The job of nourishing the canine athlete is one circumstance in which dietary supplementation may be necessary—assuming, that is, that you choose to forego a single complete and balanced diet designed specifically for this type of dog. Such supplementation should not be pursued, however, without input from a canine nutritionist or a veterinarian experienced in such matters. But regardless of what you feed and whether or not you supplement, it is important to gauge the dog's changing nutritional needs as you go along. A working sled dog, for example, probably won't

When first introducing young puppies to dry puppy food, the kibble should be moistened into a mush with water to help the youngsters ingest it efficiently.

Prescription Diets

Another discovery to come from the increase in canine nutrition research is the introduction of prescription diets. Available only from veterinarians, these foods are formulated to target such problems as food allergies, digestive problems, and kidney ailments, all of which may be more prevalent now that dogs are living longer.

When and How to Feed

Typically weighing in at about 55 to 75 pounds (25–34 kg), and native as it is to the frozen North where food was often scarce, the Samoyed evolved as a dog with a surprisingly efficient metabolism. Consequently, this high-powered sled dog is not nearly as large as one might expect, nor is it expensive or complicated to feed.

In addition to feeding the dog at the same times in the same place every day, part of developing and maintaining the dog's household routine is establishing a feeding schedule. This involves more than simply offering the dog a big bowl of food once a day and forcing it to wait 24 hours before it sees another meal.

If the dog is game, free feeding is the most convenient way to go about nourishing your pet. Here you simply ensure that there is food (preferably dry food for obvious reasons of cleanliness and odor) in the dog's dish at all times, thus allowing the dog to eat whenever it feels the desire to do so. A dog accustomed to this method is far less prone to obesity, because it eats very naturally in response to the genuine biological demands of its body.

But not all dogs, especially dogs that have had to compete with other dogs at mealtimes at some time in their lives, will cooperate with the free-feeding regimen. They just never seem to understand that the food will always be there, choosing instead to prepare for the worst and wolf down immediately

need its high-energy fuel during the summer months, because of a reduction in both activity levels and the need for energy for body warmth. Make the necessary adjustments depending on athletic activity, climate, and any other pertinent factors.

If possible, offer your dog two or three small feedings spread throughout the day rather than one large feeding once a day. This can prevent digestive problems, canine bloat, and hunger-related anxiety.

whatever they find in their dishes. Such an animal requires a different feeding strategy, preferably one in which the day's ration of food is divided into two or three feedings that are offered at two or three times during the day. Not only will this prevent the dog from feeling overcome by hunger hours after a single meal was consumed, but it can also prevent canine bloat (gastric dilation-volvulus, see page 81), a deadly condition that can strike a dog that bolts its food and/or exercises vigorously immediately after eating.

Regardless of the feeding method employed, make sure the dog's food dishes are clean, the food supplies stored properly for freshness, and make sure the dog has access to fresh, clean water at all times. You may also offer the healthy dog treats from time to time—especially during training sessions with a headstrong Samoyed that may find the sessions more interesting if some treat rewards are involved.

A word of warning: Treats can be dangerous. Never offer your pet:
• chocolate, which is toxic to dogs
• alcohol, which can kill dogs
• small, brittle bones, such as those from poultry or pork, which can lodge in the throat or digestive tract
• raw meat or eggs, which can carry salmonella

As we have seen, table scraps do not make appropriate dog treats either, due to the caloric toll they can take on a Sammy's svelte form. Superior treat choices include those formulated specifically for dogs, the choices of which can be staggering so varied are the types and flavors available. Some dogs even consider pieces of chopped vegetables to be tasty, and therefore coveted, treats, which can be especially handy, not to mention low in calories, for a dog on a diet.

And finally, when the holidays roll around and you feel inclined to invite

Just say "No" to your pet's pleadings for table scraps that can lead to digestive upset and obesity.

your pampered pet to partake of the turkey and all the trimmings, opt instead to offer it a moderate serving of canned dog food—turkey-flavored, of course. Your Sammy won't know the difference, and it will be just as pleased with its special meal as you are with yours.

While regular high-quality maintenance diets are appropriate for most dogs, a working sled dog may require a higher-energy diet and perhaps even, on the advice of a veterinarian, nutritional supplementation.

Keeping the Samoyed Beautiful

A Mantle of White

While those who know and love the Samoyed think first of this dog's inner beauty when they reflect upon the object of their affections, what attracts most people's attention upon first meeting this animal is its stunning external beauty. Arguably the most beautiful dog in the canine family, this is an animal that stops traffic every time it walks down the street. One look at its lovely white or biscuit coat, offset by black points, twinkling dark eyes, and its signature smile, and most people first question if the vision could truly be real, then vow never to forget it.

Yet the white coat that makes the Sammy the Sammy can also be a curse should the dog fall into the hands of someone who is not up to the task of caring for it. Ask those who volunteer for Samoyed breed rescue, and, sadly, many will list the care of the coat as one of the main reasons Sammies are given up to them to place in new homes. Far too many owners find they simply are not prepared or skilled enough to brush so profuse a coat down to the skin on a routine basis. They don't realize the dog will "blow its coat" once or twice a year and leave handfuls of white fluff around the house like great snow drifts left in the wake of a blizzard.

The Samoyed's coat is one of the classic double variety—a lifesaving miracle of nature that stood between the dog's survival and death in its Arctic home. Like the Sammy's temperament, its coat has remained unchanged by the course of time, shining in its silver-tipped glory today just as vibrantly as it did 100, 200, even thousands of years ago.

Two Coats in One

An engineering marvel of the highest order, this coat, as its name so accurately implies, is actually two coats in one. As one plunge of your hand into its white splendor will tell you, it consists on one level of a soft fluffy undercoat that lies close to the skin, trapping air that may then be warmed to keep the skin and the internal system it protects from winter's subzero temperatures. Protecting the downy undercoat is the second component, a mantle of longer, coarser guard hairs that repel the ice and snow that would otherwise work their way into the undercoat and saturate it and the skin with a deadly chill. When the coat "blows," once or twice a year, it is primarily the undercoat that is shed, leaving soft fluffy snowballs of hair wherever the dog wanders, making room for a fresh growth of down to take its place.

Insulation

The coat also acts to insulate the dog during the summer, although the animal must still have access to shade at all times and ideally be brought indoors when the temperatures are too warm for this tundra native to tolerate. Unfortunately, though, those fledgling owners not versed in the miraculous all-season properties of the coat automatically assume that, come summer, the coat has got to go. A Sammy whose coat has been shaved or clipped is a pathetic sight. The accompanying embarrassment in the dog's eyes reflects the fact that this intelligent animal, forced to face the world without its crowning glory, knows that such a condition is wrong!

Matting

Of course, sometimes the coat must be shaved or clipped very short, as it is prone to matting and, when neglected, will twist itself into one giant snarl that must be removed. The removal of the matted coat is usually the only remedy for such a situation, and certainly the most humane way, as de-matting instruments can be quite painful for the dog on whom they are used. The one saving grace for such a dog is the fact that the hair will indeed grow back, and the dog can once again prance proudly down the street, shrouded beautifully in the mantle of white that is its birthright.

The Home Grooming Regimen

When asked to describe the attributes of the ideal Samoyed owner, it is not at all unusual for Sammy breeders to answer in swift unison: "someone who likes to brush dogs!" Begin to attempt to add up all the hours you must spend engaged in this activity to keep the dog's coat and skin pristine and healthy, and you'll probably decide that you'd rather not know those figures after all.

Though this is a natural dog that requires nothing much more than routine brushing and combing—no fancy haircuts, no special equipment—it soon becomes clear to the new owner of an adult Samoyed in full coat just why so many owners prefer to have

their dogs tended to by professional groomers. Nevertheless, Sammy grooming can be done at home, and the following tenets will help you get through it.

Early Introductions

The earlier a Samoyed, or any dog, is introduced to the protocols of grooming, the better grooming subject it will be in the years ahead. Not that there is anything unsavory or painful about grooming that would make it something the Sam should dread, but it does require the dog to stay in one place for a while, and it may entail certain sensations to which the dog is not accustomed, therein lies the challenge.

The fun-loving Samoyed may rebel at first when it realizes that you expect it to remain lying on one side for 20 minutes, then on the other side for 20 minutes, and then be still while you pull at its tail, tend to the sensitive areas around its groin and haunches, and remain even more still as you pick and prod at its feet and clip its nails. But, as with all training—and indeed this is all part of training—introducing the dog to these experiences at an early age and keeping the sessions short and highlighted by treats, will in time cause the dog to look forward to the grooming routine as a special time that you spend together. It may even come to overlook the inordinate amount of time you expect it to tolerate your ministrations.

The Necessary Supplies

Because the Samoyed is so natural a dog in need of no extraordinary grooming efforts, you will not go broke stocking up on the necessary grooming supplies for your pet. Though its coat will demand much of your time, its fundamental grooming needs, and thus the commensurate grooming supplies, are simple in kind, economical in price.

Only the properly groomed Samoyed can exude the profound beauty for which this breed is known.

Brushes and combs. Brushing and combing comprise the majority of the Sammy's coat care, so tools for those activities are the primary equipment items you will need. Opinions vary on the optimum brush for a Sam, but purchase both a pin brush (an oval brush with metal bristles that resemble the heads of pins) and a slicker brush (a rectangular field of slender curved

Brushes, a rake, and nail clippers are the primary pieces of equipment you will need to keep your Sammy beautiful.

metal bristles that is expert at removing dead and loose hair), as there will probably be moments when you deem that one or the other is better for the coat at a given time. The comb, too, is a staple in the Samoyed grooming kit, as are a rake to remove loose hair, a good pair of well-constructed toenail clippers designed for large dogs with large nails, blood-stopping powder should you accidentally clip a nail too close to the quick, a pet toothbrush and toothpaste formulated specifically for dogs, and a supply of dog shampoo for bathtime (some Sammy owners use shampoos made especially for white dogs; others prefer conditioning or flea shampoos).

Grooming accessories. As for the accessories, gather up a collection of old towels and perhaps blankets, too, all of which will be permanently designated as belonging to your pet for a variety of uses from impromptu bedding to bath toweling to grooming mats. And finally, don't forget the diversions. It's always wise to have treats and/or special toys handy to divert the dog's attention during grooming. Some dogs feel suddenly inclined to chew in the midst of a rigorous brushing session; offer such a dog a favorite rope toy to vent the built-up anxiety and energy. Or perhaps your pet doesn't particularly enjoy nail clipping. Have some treats ready to reward the dog for complying with your requests that it sit still and offer its paws willingly for this less-than-coveted procedure.

Routine Coat Care

Brushing and combing; that about sums up the grooming practices required to keep the Samoyed healthy in coat. Routine brushing, as simple a procedure as it is, can work miracles. It distributes the oils in the coat and skin; it removes dead hair that can not only be annoying calling cards all over your house and in your food, but also cause hot spots and other skin problems; it prevents the mats to which the Samoyed's coat is so prone; it keeps both hair and skin healthy—and all while it is performing its preventive miracles, the actual act of brushing is immensely pleasurable for the dog, or at least it should be.

Aside from the simplicity of the Sammy grooming routine, prospective owners are to be warned, and current owners reminded, that that thick white coat must be brushed and combed completely—every part of the body down to the skin—at least once a week, and preferably more often. This can be done in a single session, or, if your own demanding schedule precludes your ability to set aside the hour or more that this requires each week, you can divide the dog's body into sections and concentrate on one section each or every other day.

The Samoyed is blessed with a double coat that helped to insulate it from even the most frigid Arctic temperatures.

However you choose to groom your Sam, whichever method meshes best with your household rhythms, what is universal for all is the fact that the job must be done thoroughly. Sure it's

Those who choose the Samoyed as a pet must commit to a regimen of diligent care of that great white coat. Only those who truly enjoy brushing dogs should apply.

easy just to glide the brush over the top layer of guard hairs, smoothing them down and conveniently ignoring the brushing needs of the soft, mat-prone undercoat beneath, but this is of no benefit to the dog, who in no time will be riddled with mats and a variety of other skin and coat problems borne of neglect. If you don't have the time, or the job proves to be too intimidating, then by all means get the dog to the groomer. Delivering your dog into the care of a trained professional for this responsibility is superior to giving up and sending the dog off to the animal shelter or into the home of a new owner.

Technique. The proper way to brush a Samoyed involves first addressing a particular section of hair, for instance, that over the dog's ribs on the right side. Ideally, the dog should lie down on its left side, a position that offers you liberal access to the area you will be brushing. Brush first against the grain of the hair, so to speak, to remove the dead and loose clumps of undercoat hiding beneath

An important prerequisite for Samoyed ownership is a willingness to spend a great deal of time brushing this lushly coated dog.

the guard hairs. Once you believe you have thoroughly brushed this area, reverse direction and brush the guard hairs back with the direction of their growth.

If you will be brushing the entire dog in a single session, you may choose to brush against the grain first from head to toe, then with the grain for the final touch. However you do it, pay close attention to the area behind the ears, around the tail, the groin, and under the elbows, as these are all prime territory for mat formation (and for flea colonization). If you do find budding mats that you cannot simply brush or comb out with little discomfort to the dog, feel free to cut them out. This should not create any large gaps of hair in the regularly tended coat, and it is the quickest and least painful way to remove mats from the Sammy coat.

Shedding. Be warned, too, that once or twice a year your Sam will "blow" its coat, usually in the spring and possibly in the fall, as well. The undercoat will come out in great fistfuls of fluff, and your job as Sammy groomer will become even more demanding. During this period of time, daily brushing is a must and weekly bathing a help, for the released coat must be collected to prevent mats, skin problems, and wads of hair all over the house and the yard. Coat blowing is far more dramatic in intact Samoyeds, as spayed or neutered Sams are more inclined to shed gradually throughout the year than in one fell swoop. Either way, the coat must be tended to, and tended to with dedication.

While it does require a substantial investment of time on your part, if you choose to be your Samoyed's own in-house groomer, you are in for some unexpected surprises. As time goes by and you establish your routine, you will one day realize that this, too, is contributing to the bond between you and your pet. You may find that you look forward to the time you set aside for your weekly grooming sessions, especially if the rest of the week has been filled with non-dog-related demands and stress. The grooming session offers you both a break from the hysteria, an opportunity to sit together and enjoy the sensation of the brush and comb running through lovely white hair, to watch TV, to talk about your day, to enjoy each other's company. Allow this to become a special bonding ritual that you would never dream of giving up.

Bathtime

Samoyeds are not what one would call water-loving dogs in the tradition of the Golden or Labrador Retrievers (to be saturated with water in the Arctic meant death), yet most will tolerate the water when it's time for a bath. Now, the owner of a dog with such a dense white double coat is not likely to relish the thought of attempting to saturate that coat down to the skin and then ensuring that every sud is rinsed from its strands, but that is the challenge that lies ahead as you prepare the bath. Here, too, don't discount the availability of the professional groomer, who is trained in such matters and has the equipment available to make the job easier.

Fortunately, bathing that coat is necessary only occasionally, usually every two or three months. Mother Nature apparently knew that a dog of such white and ivory splendor must be blessed with a coat that is somewhat self-cleaning, and indeed that is what you will find with the Samoyed (also, the coat lacks the traditional "doggy" odor that most dogs share).

Bathing Indoors or Outdoors

Bathing at home can be carried out in a number of ways. Your own bathtub can act as a fine Sammy tub (with a rubber mat on the tub floor to pre-

vent Sammy paws from slipping on slick porcelain or fiberglass), but in summer you may prefer to bathe the dog outdoors to prevent the need for a massive post-Sammy-bath cleanup following the big event. Another clever option for outdoor bathing is to transform a large plastic (clean) trashcan or children's pool into a bathtub. Fill the receptacle with lukewarm water, lift your pet into it, and you will be amazed at how quickly and easily this enables you to thoroughly saturate the dog's coat. Then take the now wet dog out of its makeshift tub, lather up the coat and use a garden hose with a light spray for the rinse.

Preparations Before Bathing

However you choose to bathe the dog, proper preparation will make the job proceed much more smoothly. Gather all the supplies you will need— shampoo, towels, washcloths—and keep them within easy reach of the bathing site. Run the bath, and then go fetch the dog, who may at that moment, having witnessed the preparations, be hiding under the bed.

While most Samoyeds won't take to the water like a Labrador Retriever, they will usually tolerate the bath, especially if they are introduced to bathing at a young age.

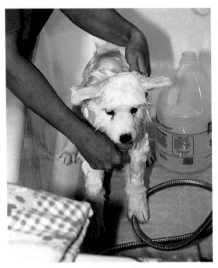

The bath begins with thorough saturation with water down to the skin.

Beware: Once or twice a year, the Samoyed will "blow" its undercoat and leave what looks like a freshly fallen blanket of snow in your home and yard.

Before you begin the bath, a good brushing is in order to unravel any budding mats. Cut out any existing mats that you find, as these will only tighten with the bath.

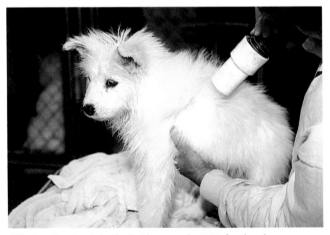

Whether the dog is bathed at home or by a professional groomer, making sure that the coat has been thoroughly dried—which can take all day, even with the help of a blow dryer or professional drying equipment—is a critical step in the procedure.

Technique for Bathing

Once you have the dog in the tub, tackle the job of getting that coat saturated to the skin. In time you will learn how to do this most efficiently for your dog's own particular tastes. For instance, some dogs don't mind being bathed from neck to tail to toe, yet balk at having a wet head and ears. For such a dog, wash the rest of the body first, and save cleaning of the face and ears for last (you may want to place cotton balls in the ears to prevent water from seeping in). Now apply the shampoo, which should also be worked in down to the skin.

The next step is the most difficult, and the most time-consuming: the rinse. You must ensure that every last bubble is removed from the dog's coat and skin, as soap residue can dry and irritate the skin. Even when you believe you have accomplished your task and not a sud of soap remains, rinse again just to be sure. When you no longer see soap or bubbles falling from the

Because the optimum lifestyle for the Samoyed calls for a great deal of time spent outdoors, the control of fleas and ticks must be taken very seriously.

dog, rinse one more time. If you have reserved the washing of the dog's face and head for the end, wash the head with a drop of shampoo and the face with a clean washcloth and water.

Now fully bathed, the dog's natural inclination will be to shake, and the amount of water that can cling to a coat of this type is phenomenal. You will see this with the first shake as you and everything in the vicinity is suddenly as saturated as the dog. One way to reduce the flood, is to snap on the dog's leash and take it outdoors to do its shaking (a natural task if you are already outdoors, of course). The key word here, however, is "leash." The dog that is allowed to run loose and shake is also the dog that is likely to begin rolling in the grass or even a mud puddle to remove the strange scents from its coat, and then you must start all over again.

Drying

Your next task is to towel dry the dog gently from head to foot. If you dry the face and head first, the dog may be less inclined to roll, more inclined to cooperate with your drying and brushing efforts. Complete drying can take an entire day, so make sure the dog remains somewhere in the home or outdoors where it is safe from catching a chill; perhaps help accelerate the process by taking a warm (not hot) blow dryer to the coat (most successful if you have previously introduced the blow dryer to the dog and convinced it that this strange and rather noisy machine poses no threat). Brush the dog periodically throughout the day to remove the hairs that are inevitably released by the bathing process, and soon your dog will be just as clean, dry, and sweet-smelling as it is beautiful. You'll both be quite pleased.

HOW-TO:
Care of the Eyes, Ears, and Teeth

The well-groomed Sam cannot live by brushing and bathing alone. Its ears, eyes, and teeth also require a bit of routine attention. By offering that, you not only keep every nook and cranny of the dog's body clean, but you may also uncover a budding health problem that may be easily vanquished in the early stages.

Ear Care

Given the structure of the Samoyed's ears, infections and other such problems here are rare. The dog's erect prick ears allow ample air circulation that thus prevents the buildup of moisture that can so plague floppy-eared dogs.

Nevertheless, the Samoyed's ears, too, deserve and need your attention to keep potential problems at bay.

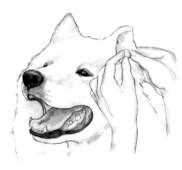

Because their erect construction fosters air circulation, maintenance of the Samoyed's ears is relatively simple.

• The first step is to keep your eye, or rather, your nose, on the ears. Stick your nose into your dog's ears and take a whiff. You may feel a bit silly, but this is the only way you will learn what the animal's healthy ear should smell like. Because ear infections and problems often manifest in a strange odor that emanates from the ear canal, by getting acquainted with the scent of the healthy ear you are better equipped to detect the genesis of an unhealthy ear later on.

• Watch for telltale signs of ear discomfort. If the dog begins shaking its head or pawing at an ear incessantly, it is trying to tell you something; take a look at its ears. The culprit may be a flea tickling the ear flap as it meanders through the hairs, or it may be far more serious, such as an embedded foxtail or an infection. Get the dog to the veterinarian for a more complete examination.

• Keep the ears clean at home. Be warned, however, that your job is to clean the ear flaps only, never the delicate interior of the ear, which can be severely damaged if you poke and prod the canal with foreign objects. The ear cleaning with which you must be concerned is occasionally swabbing the inner ear flaps with mineral oil on a cotton ball. This will keep the skin clean and prevent it from overdrying.

• In your examinations of your pet's ears, you may find a profuse growth of hair at the entrance to each ear canal. The hair grows here as a protective measure, keeping insects, dust, and other would-be infiltrators out of the ear's inner recesses. On some dogs, however, the hair is too thick, in which case the veterinarian may advise you to trim the area a bit to prevent that dreaded buildup of moisture. If you are not so advised, leave the ears alone.

Eye Care

The Samoyed's eyes require more observation than outright care, but because the windows to the soul may also react to health problems elsewhere in the body, it is the wise owner who keeps a close eye on his or her dog's peepers.

• Look periodically into your dog's eyes for a dull or opaque cast to the corneas. While cataracts or eyelash abnormalities can cause signs that indicate actual damage to the eyeball itself, more common is a sudden discharge from the eyes. This may be nothing more than a very visible sign of a simple pollen allergy or the result of a minor malformation of the eye's structure—or it could be the sign of something more serious either in the eye or elsewhere in the body.

• Have runny eyes or any suspicious eye symptom examined by a veterinarian, preferably a practitioner who specializes in veterinary ophthalmology. Sympathetic as you are likely to be to your dog's red, runny eyes, resist the temptation to alleviate such symptoms with drops or ointments made for human eyes unless you are specifically instructed to do so by a veterinarian.

Tooth Care

Once upon a time, dogs lived to the ripe old age of nine or ten, just the age when the teeth, after a long life of dedicated service, would begin to give out. Today that canine lifespan has extended into the teens, thus exposing a great many of our dogs to such conditions as canine gum disease, which were unheard of 30 years ago. Tooth care has thus become an important element in the realm of both grooming and general dog care.

• Have your pet's teeth cleaned professionally by the veterinarian twice a year, and brush the dog's teeth daily or every other day at home, and you can help your companion keep its teeth, or at least most of them, well into its golden years. The concept of canine toothbrushing is fairly contemporary, and there are still those who scoff at the idea. But the resulting clean teeth, fresh breath, and a full set of choppers are well worth the effort.

• Begin by gathering your supplies: a pet toothbrush and toothpaste formulated especially for dogs (human toothpastes can burn a dog's mouth and cause gastric upset).

• Place the paste on the brush, pull the corner of the Samoyed's lips back and out with your fin-

Once it is accustomed to tooth-brushing, the dog should begin to enjoy both the sensation of the brush on its gums and the taste of the toothpaste that is formulated especially for the canine palate.

ger, and take the pasted brush to the newly exposed back molars.

• Brush in a circular motion to address both teeth and gums, and work your way forward to the teeth in front. Then, start all over again, back molars first, on the other side of the mouth.

It sounds so easy, yet this is obviously not a natural activity for a dog, and even the fun-lov-

ing, adventure-seeking Samoyed may practically laugh out loud at your intention of placing this strange stick in its mouth. If this is your dog's reaction, appeal to its curiosity. Allow it to sniff and lick the toothbrush, and before even attempting to brush the teeth, squeeze a dab of toothpaste on your finger and offer it to the dog for a taste. Most dogs enjoy the meat or other flavoring with which the paste is laced, and will thus gladly cooperate with your subsequent attempts to brush the stuff all over their teeth.

It may take a few sessions to convince your dog that you mean well and that this is actually an enjoyable activity, but most dogs eventually come around. Even if grudgingly, they seem to realize and acknowledge that they enjoy the sensation of toothbrushing and actually feel better when it's done. Of course they'll feel even better when they are afforded the luxury of greeting the aging process with all their teeth intact, but that is a benefit of toothbrushing that even the intelligent Samoyed will never be able to understand.

Fighting Fleas and Ticks

Fleas

Every spring a horror movie of sorts opens throughout the nation. The villains are blood-sucking parasitic insects that hop aboard their victims—which are often canine—and make themselves and their offspring at home for the duration. These tiny bloodsuckers are, of course, fleas, resilient little creatures with hardy constitutions and phenomenally quick and efficient reproduction rates. When you understand the facts about fleas, you will have taken your first important step toward claiming the title of first-class flea fighter and defender of the dog.

The battle that awaits you rages on three fronts: the dog, your home (which includes your furniture, your carpet, your bed, your dog's bed, and everything else within your house walls), and the yard. A variety of products are available for each of these theaters of war, but only those that are compatible with one another should be used, and all should be used only as directed. Consult your veterinarian before launching this potentially very frustrating mission, and make sure the products you will be using are safe and effective.

The best plan is to begin by bathing and perhaps flea-dipping and/or spraying the dog (all with compatible prod-

A tick before and after a meal.

ucts, of course). With the dog out of the house, perhaps having been delivered into the hands of a qualified groomer for de-fleaing, you may attack the house and yard with flea bombs, sprays, whatever types of products you have chosen. Your goal for the dog is to remove the fleas that have taken up residence on its skin and in its coat. If you spot one flea either on the dog or somewhere in your house, you know there are more, not just on the dog, but throughout its environment, and your environment, as well. As for that environment, your goal is to kill all of the adult and preadult (eggs and larvae) fleas hiding there, so choose products that are up to the task but that do not pose a threat to your pet.

When you have finished this particular battle, you may rest briefly on your laurels, but be prepared to take up arms again in a few weeks, especially if you are waging the war during summer, prime flea season. Unfortunately, however, in some areas, prime flea season is every season.

While life in the Arctic was not typically conducive to flea infestations of the resident Sammies, these parasites can indeed be a scourge to contemporary Sams, especially those in more temperate climates that foster year-round flea populations. In most areas, winter's chill either destroys the summer's fleas, or at least urges them into hibernation, but in some areas, the battle must be fought all year long. There is hope, however. In the never-ending search for the perfect end-all flea eradicator, recent discoveries in the flea-control laboratory have led to the development of several new types of products with that promise. One is a new oral prescription remedy that prevents preadult fleas from maturing, and thus, of course, reproducing. Another, also available by prescription, is applied to a single spot on the dog and kills resident fleas for weeks.

A close-up of the most common, most frustrating, external parasite to affect the dog: the flea.

In the meantime, however, it is wise to continue on the three-prong attack method of flea control and to consult with your veterinarian to devise the most effective and safest program for your individual pet.

Ticks

While dealing with fleas can be frustrating enough, yet another external parasite that is ever hungry for your dog's blood is the tick, a small round pest that has ample access to a dog as outdoorsy as the Samoyed. The two typically meet in wooded areas where the dog is hiking, backpacking, sledding, or partaking in any such fun activity it enjoys with its owner. It then returns home with an uninvited guest: a tick that has latched on and grows gradually more obese as it feasts on the dog's blood.

It is thus to your dog's benefit to do a thorough examination of the animal as soon as you arrive home, your mission being to seek and destroy any unwanted souvenirs that may have hitched a ride. This is not an easy job, especially if the dog is in full coat, but ticks can carry such potentially serious illnesses as canine ehrlichiosis, Rocky Mountain spotted fever, and Lyme disease, the latter of which is considered the most common tick-borne illness, resulting in arthritislike joint pain, lameness, weakness, and fever. Ticks should not, therefore, be allowed to feast at will.

If you do find a tick latched onto your pet's skin, grasp securely as much of its engorged body as you can with a pair of tweezers or between your thumb and forefinger, then slowly and smoothly pull the tick out. Apply antibiotic ointment to the site and watch for the next few weeks for signs of joint stiffness, apathy, weight loss, lethargy, or respiratory congestion that could indicate the onset of a tick-borne illness.

While the image of a rotund tick embedding its head into your Sammy's skin is hardly pleasant, the good news is that a sound flea-control program often targets the tick, as well. Choose flea-control products with this dual-purpose action, remain true to that primary battle against the flea, and you may never even have to ponder the idea of waging war against the equally bloodthirsty tick.

For a further discussion of fleas and ticks, see page 83.

Caring for the Feet and Nails

Foot Care

Historically, the Samoyed's feet were of critical importance to the dog's survival. Not only did they have to be of the proper structure to traverse the ever-changing Arctic tundra, but they also had to be tough and well-furred to withstand the terrain and frigid temperatures. Today's Samoyed remains blessed with those well-engineered feet, though the demands on their performance are not quite as rigorous as they once were.

• It will be imperative through the years for you to handle your dog's feet—to check for a buildup of ice between the toes, to clip the nails, or to clean a small pad abrasion sustained while hiking—so, as soon as possible start playing with the pup's feet and get it used to the sensation. Then, when serious business is in order, the dog will see nothing out of the ordinary in your attentions to these important appendages.

• Where grooming is concerned, you must address two separate areas of the foot. First, the soft tissues. An outdoorsy Sam's feet are prone to damage from foxtails, ice balls, salt, and glass shards, all of which may worm their way into the delicate skin between the toes or even into the tougher skin of the pads, and cause great pain and

Nail clipping can be a challenge, so it is best to introduce the dog to the procedure at a young age, and take great care to clip only the tip of the nail and avoid the blood-rich quick.

injury to the unsuspecting pup. You must thus examine the feet for these intruders regularly and thoroughly, especially after every foray into the great outdoors, and especially if your dog suddenly begins to limp.

Nail Care

Related of course to the foot-care agenda are the toenails. If you allow them to grow unchecked, they can severely hinder the dog's ability to walk and move correctly and comfortably. The nails of a dog that walks frequently on hard surfaces will be somewhat filed down by the constant friction between nail and ground, but they will still require trimming. The same holds true for the dewclaws, the nails that grow up near the ankle and never have contact with the ground. Most breeders have their puppies' dewclaws removed within several days of their birth, but if your dog's dewclaws are intact, you must keep them trimmed to prevent pain and injury to your pet.

Many owners pale at the thought of taking on the job of nail trimming by themselves. For such owners, professional groomers are well prepared to take up that slack every month or two to keep the nails trimmed at the proper length. But in truth, there is nothing to fear from nail clipping as long as you proceed carefully and patiently, and help your dog adjust along the way.

• Once again, early acclimation is the most effective step toward successful nail trimming. The dog that learns to tolerate the procedure as a puppy will have no trouble dealing with it gracefully as an adult, assuming, of course, its formative experiences are positive. You can ensure they are so by first understanding the structure of the nail. Take care, for example, to trim only the lighter outside rim of the nail and avoid the darker blood-rich quick that lies close to the toe, as the quick will bleed profusely if nicked. (Apply blood-stopping powder or a styptic pencil if you do "quick" the dog; it happens even to the best of professionals.) If the dog has black nails that prevent you from discerning the tip from the quick, clip only the very tip, and trim the nails every week or so rather than every month to ensure that you not only keep them short enough, but also avoid the potential bloodletting.

• Positive associations may be further encouraged by bribing the dog with treats. Depending on the dog's opinion of nail clipping, you may be able to do all the nails on all the feet in one sitting, after which the dog is rewarded with the much-coveted treat. More likely, however, is the possibility that your dog will not be so amenable, so be patient. In this case you may need to clip only a few nails per sitting, the dog receiving a treat after each nail. Do what you have to do to get the job done.

The Healthy, Happy Samoyed

A Healthy Lifestyle

By all rights, the name "Samoyed" should be synonymous with the word "health." This is a dog born and bred for a life of athletic effort as well as companionship with the human species, and to accomplish these goals, the Sam must be healthy.

Hailing as it does from the top of the world, the most treacherous terrain and climate the world has to offer, the law of survival of the fittest was in play each and every day of the Samoyed's evolution. The dog that could not withstand the cold, food shortages, and rigorous work schedule pulling sleds and herding reindeer—standard everyday challenges of life in the Arctic— would not survive to pass on its genetic material to future generations. On the other hand, the dog that met these challenges with health and aplomb was the dog that was chosen for procreation. It is thus the health and well-being of that latter dog's progeny that we are entrusted with today.

The key to upholding the covenant our species made with the Samoyed ages ago is to commit to instituting a healthy lifestyle for the dog from puppyhood on. The components of this are rooted in common sense, and, in fact, apply to humans as well as to dogs. A healthy, high-quality diet free of table scraps and other unhealthy, obesity-causing agents, regular daily exercise, routine veterinary care and the commensurate vaccinations, and plenty of loving, stimulating companionship; this is what the healthy Samoyed is made of.

This program of good health can prove quite a challenge to an owner who was originally carried away by the enthusiasm that an adorable bearlike Samoyed puppy can inspire, only to feel the fire dwindle as the dog matures and the weight of the commitment grows heavier than this ill-prepared owner expected. This may all be avoided by learning about that commitment ahead of time, pledging to the reality of it, and, in doing so, reaping the vast benefits of it that, for the right owner, far outweigh the time, effort, and often even the hassle involved. The result will be a healthy dog that lives to a ripe old age—and perhaps a healthier owner, as well.

When seeking a veterinarian for your pet, evaluate the attitude of the support staff as well as the doctor, and the overall atmosphere of the office.

The Veterinarian's Role

The healthy Samoyed cannot reap the benefits of good health in a vacuum. The dog requires not only a commitment to health from its owner, but also the attentions of a skilled veterinarian, who, ideally, will work in partnership with the owner to ensure that the dog receives the finest care possible.

Unfortunately, all veterinarians, like all dog owners, are not created equal, so the owner must choose his or her pet's doctor carefully. This begins by asking dog-owning friends, trainers, local dog clubs, and humane societies for recommendations. A community's dog-owning network is usually well-aware of which veterinarians are the tops, and most are pleased to share that knowledge with others.

Your Personal Evaluation

Once you have the name of a likely candidate, take the dog in for an examination and pay close attention to the operation of the office. Notice, for example, the reception personnel. Are they polite, competent, and gentle with both the animals and their owners? Is the facility clean and well-organized? Do you notice a large number of repeat clients and the staff's personal knowledge of their pets?

Of utmost importance, of course, is the veterinarian, and the first step here is observing carefully how he or she interacts with your dog. A Samoyed boasts a universal love for most humans, even those dressed in white coats with stethoscopes around their necks, and few people can resist this dog's gregariously affectionate nature. But you should still be able to gauge the veterinarian's response to your dog by the way he or she talks to and touches the animal.

• Ideal is the veterinarian who has committed to this calling out of a pure

In honoring the ancient tradition of Samoyed ownership, ensure that your pet is offered a healthy diet, plenty of exercise, and ample doses of love and affection every day of its life.

Choose a veterinarian with whom both you and your dog are comfortable—and one who exhibits a genuine love for dogs.

A puppy's initial series of vaccinations should begin when the youngster is weaned, at about five or six weeks of age.

and unwavering love for animals; such motivations are usually evident from the first few moments of the doctor's meeting a new patient.

• Veterinary care can be expensive, so you want a veterinarian who is sensitive to this and prescribes what is best for the pet, even if this cannot be inflated to provide hefty profits to the veterinarian.

• You want someone who will be sensitive to your pet's pain and confusion, as well, and dedicated to instituting a solid prevention program.

• You want a veterinarian who views the health of the dog holistically, acknowledging the importance of diet, exercise, athletic conditioning, and the patient's emotional outlook just as highly as that of veterinary medical care.

• You want someone who is willing and eager to answer your questions, and is pleased to explain even the most tedious details about a dog's condition and treatment.

• And finally, you want a veterinarian with whom both you and your dog are comfortable. While your dog may never actually enjoy visiting the veterinarian's office, it's comforting to know that some effort will be made by the professional staff to help ease its stress a bit. When you find such an individual, that person, and the role he or she will play in the long-term health of your canine companion, will prove through the years to be more precious than gold.

A Partnership

A solid partnership between the dog's veterinarian and its owner is the first step toward a sound preventive medicine program, as well. The owner relies on the veterinarian's skills as a diagnostician and informational source, while the veterinarian relies on the owner to remain attuned to

Your pet's initial series of puppy vaccinations and its annual boosters are the most important elements in its long-term preventive medicine program.

his or her pet at home, aware of what is normal for the dog and what isn't. On that inevitable day when the dog just isn't right, it may be referred quickly to the veterinarian for treatment that may be more successful because the offending condition is caught early. In the long run, it is the dog that emerges the victor from such a partnership.

Routine Vaccinations

Advancements in veterinary medicine have reached a fever pitch in recent years, thanks in part to the increasing credibility our society has been willing to assign the bond between people and their pets. One area that has benefited greatly from this trend is that of preventive medicine. At the heart of the dog's long-term preventive medicine program are its vaccinations. If you neglect them, a single fatal bout of parvovirus or distemper could leave you wishing that you had taken the need for vaccinations more seriously.

The vaccinations begin during early puppyhood, with a puppy's first vaccination at six to eight weeks of age, followed by a series of three more administered every three weeks there-

after. There is a method to this madness: Before the puppy is weaned from its mother's milk, it is Mom's maternal antibodies that protect her pups from disease. But we can never be sure when the maternal antibodies in the puppy's system relinquish control of the youngster's immunity to the vaccine antibodies, and it is not unusual for maternal antibodies to react against the artificially introduced vaccines and render them useless. The series, then, is essentially an insurance policy that the vaccine is finally effective amid the uncertainty of the presence of maternal antibodies.

Puppy Vaccinations

The classic puppy vaccination is a combination designed to prevent:
• hepatitis (an infectious viral illness that affects the liver, kidneys, and blood vessels)
• parvovirus (a severe, extremely contagious viral illness that most commonly attacks the gastrointestinal tract and frequently claims the lives of puppies)
• leptospirosis (a bacterial illness that most often affects the kidneys and causes a hunched-up appearance in the affected dog)
• distemper (a highly contagious viral illness that may affect any number of tissues and is probably responsible for more canine deaths worldwide than any other disease)
• parainfluenza (a viral illness involved in what is known as the kennel cough complex that is associated with respiratory infections)
• canine coronavirus (a viral illness similar to, though not quite as severe as, parvovirus).

Given the severity and potentially deadly nature of these illnesses, the initial series is then followed by annual boosters every year for the remainder of the dog's life. Many veterinarians now also recommend an additional parvovirus vaccination for puppies of five to six months of age, as the maternal antibodies against parvo may remain in the puppy's system for an inordinate period of time. This extra vaccination won't hurt the puppy, and it may actually protect it from an adolescent case of this serious, life-threatening disease.

Rabies Vaccination

One vaccination that is not included in the puppy series (other than the optional vaccinations for such illnesses as Lyme disease and kennel cough) is the rabies vaccination. Unlike the vaccinations for the other common canine illnesses, the rabies vaccination is mandated by law in most communities. It cannot be administered until the puppy reaches four months of age, with boosters every one or three years thereafter, depending on the particular vaccination. While the rabies vaccination is typically a requisite for licensing dogs in most communities, it is also a common-sense "must" for a dog, especially for the very active Samoyed, which spends a great deal of time outdoors. If you neglect to protect this gregarious animal from this disease that attacks the brain and is 100 percent fatal, you will live to regret that neglect when the dog attempts to play tag with an infected skunk or raccoon and is bitten during the activity!

Early Diagnosis of Disease

Sometimes, despite the best intentions, despite routine vaccinations, despite diligent attention to the dog's health, a Sammy begins to behave in an uncharacteristically quiet, despondent mood, uninterested in food, water, or playmates. Any drastic change in demeanor or activity level should be heeded just as seriously as blatant physical symptoms, and should be reported to the dog's veterinarian as soon as possible. The owner thus plays a critical role in the early diagnosis of illness and injury, his or her daily observations of the dog at home being the first step to getting the dog to the veterinarian for diagnosis and treatment.

Home evaluations are the key to early diagnosis, which may in turn be the key to saving a dog's life. It's no secret that for the vast majority of conditions that can affect dogs (and humans, too), the patient has a much better chance of recovering, not to mention surviving, if the condition is diagnosed early in its development and treated before treatment is rendered ineffective by the severity of the condition.

Home examinations require the pet owner to get to know intimately the dog's personality, physical attributes, and daily rhythms. Watch for changes in behavior, changes in urinary habits, even changes in feces consistency. Routine grooming sessions provide the optimum opportunity to check for lumps, bumps, sore spots, poor coat and skin quality, and external parasites. Other classic signs of canine health problems include:
- a loss of appetite
- pale mucous membranes
- excess thirst and urination
- limping or stiffness
- diarrhea (especially diarrhea tinged with blood, which requires immediate veterinary attention)

While every dog may at one time or another experience temporary bouts of diarrhea, appetite loss, lethargy, or the like, anything that lasts for longer than a day or two requires at least a telephone call to the veterinarian. Acute illnesses usually make their presence known quite clearly, especially when the victim is a Samoyed, a breed not typically known for stoicism in the face of illness. This very communicative dog is not likely to hide its symptoms behind a brave front; it is

Spaying and neutering helps dogs live longer, healthier, and with a deeper bond to their families.

more apt to cling to you and plead for help with its dark expressive eyes. In return, it never hurts to consult the veterinarian, even if the situation proves to be a false alarm. That consultation could save your pet's life.

The Spayed or Neutered Sam

When seeking a veterinarian to care for your beloved pet from puppyhood through old age, evaluate the doctor's perspective on breeding, as well as on spaying and neutering. Study after study proves that an altered dog, male or female, especially when altered during puppyhood, is destined to live

longer than its intact counterpart, and destined to be a better pet, as well.

Myths abound about the effects of spaying and neutering. We hear that an altered pet is fat, lazy, and inactive. False, false, false! Whether altered or intact, a dog will be fat and lazy if it is fed too much, is fed inappropriate food, and is not offered ample daily opportunities to expend its energy reserves. If you intend to keep this high-powered sled dog ensconced in the house 24 hours a day, seven days a week, yes, you will end up with a fat Samoyed that is unable even to withstand a brief walk around the neighborhood. There are few sights sadder than a beautiful though over-weight Sam walking with its tongue lolling out, its head down, its lush, plumed tail dragging between its legs rather than carried high like a banner over its back. This dog requires balance in both diet and activity, and that has nothing to do with reproductive hormones.

On the other hand, the dog that is spayed or neutered, free as it is of those pesky hormones that keep it ever attentive to signals from potential mates, is far more apt to direct its full attention to its family. Free of that uncontrollable desire to reproduce, this dog is less likely to wander away in search of other dogs, it is more likely to pay attention during training sessions, and it will be most happy sharing every minute of its day in partnership with its family.

The life of the altered pet is also more fulfilling because of the positive effects of spaying and neutering on the canine lifespan. The spayed female will not be prone to mammary cancer and various painful uterine diseases, and the neutered male will not succumb to, among others, testicular cancer and anal tumors.

But, in addition to the health benefits of spaying and neutering, altering is also the responsible choice for any pet owner. The sad fact is that the world today is plagued by an overpopulation of dogs of both pure and mixed breeding, and far too few good homes to go around. Even the lovable, adorable, effervescent Samoyed is not immune to this plague, a fact to which Samoyed breed rescue groups and animal shelters from coast to coast can attest.

The bottom line: A female Sam need not have "just one litter" before she is spayed to enjoy a full and productive life, and a male Sam will live happily ever after—probably happier ever after—without ever siring a brood of his own. What is even more important, the family pet should not be viewed as a profit-making venture or a vehicle to teach the kids "the miracle of life," leaving the resulting puppies to face an uncertain future, an unknown fate. What this dog needs is a devoted family that takes it into its heart as a family member, pure and simple. Once you choose to live with a Samoyed, extending your special years together as long as possible should be your mission. Isn't it wonderful that these two surgical procedures, two quintessential preventive measures in the quest for canine health, combined with a healthy lifestyle, will help you do just that?

Common Canine Ailments

While health and proper care go hand in hand, no dog is totally immune from illness and disease. We can work to reduce the likelihood of such problems, but there are no guarantees. The dog owner is thus wise to brush up on some of the most common ailments and conditions that can affect this species, as such knowledge is the front line of defense, first in identifying possible disorders, then in pursuing effective treatment.

Virtually every young puppy should be dewormed to protect it from internal parasites that can take a heavy toll on a young canine system.

Canine Bloat

One of the most devastating conditions that can strike a dog is canine bloat, also known as gastric dilitation-volvulus. Upon noticing the signs of this condition—restlessness, unsuccessful attempts to defecate or vomit, a bloating of the abdomen, excessive salivation, and obvious pain—get the dog to the veterinarian *as soon as possible,* or it will soon lapse into shock. Without immediate emergency attention, the dog will die.

Canine bloat is caused by a buildup of gasses and fluid in the dog's stomach. Ultimately, as the condition progresses, the stomach will rotate and constrict the circulatory system. While this is a medical emergency, even quick treatment will not guarantee survival. Depending on the severity of the given case, the veterinarian will try to release the buildup in the stomach. If this is unsuccessful, surgery is in order.

Because treatment is so unpredictable, prevention is the best weapon against canine bloat; this revolves around the dog's eating habits. Although this condition is most frequently associated with large dogs, any dog can fall victim to bloat, including the Samoyed. A sound prevention program consists of feeding the dog two or three small meals throughout the day rather than one large meal, and preventing the dog from wolfing down its food and drinking copious amounts of water right after eating. Equally helpful, especially for an active, athletic dog like the Samoyed, is to avoid feeding the dog after a vigorous exercise session. Allow its system to settle before introducing a stomach full of food.

In a multidog household, perhaps one occupied by an entire sled team, where the canine residents may gulp down dinner quickly for fear that the other dogs will appropriate their food for themselves, dogs should be fed separately and in individual dishes. Then, just to be on the safe side, keep the dog or dogs near you after mealtimes to make sure no signs begin to emerge.

Hip Dysplasia

Unfortunately, every breed is plagued with a roster of hereditary conditions that are passed on genetically from generation to generation. The Samoyed is relatively healthy in this respect, but it is not entirely free of problems.

Hip dysplasia is one condition that affects all dogs, including the Samoyed. Attempts have been made to eradicate the condition, which is a malformation of the dog's hip joint and may vary in severity from dog to dog, but this is a voluntary program and dysplastic dogs continue to be bred by people who refuse to acknowledge the magnitude of the problem. Nevertheless, only those dogs that have been X-rayed at age two and deemed clear of dysplasia by the Orthopedic Foundation for Animals

should be bred, and Sammy buyers should purchase only puppies and dogs that come from OFA-certified parents.

Hip dysplasia, which may not become evident until the dog matures, can be extremely painful to its victim, and can certainly bring an end to a promising sledding career. Depending on the severity of the condition, it can be controlled with painkillers or treated with rather drastic surgical procedures, but sometimes the only remedy to easing the dog's pain is euthanasia. The preferred course of action, then, is to work to prevent it from occurring in the first place—and in convincing others to join this mission, as well.

Kennel Cough

Dogs that are boarded frequently, dogs that compete in obedience trials, conformation shows, sled dog races, and the like, and any dog that comes in frequent contact with others of its own kind may be prone to kennel cough, also known as canine cough, known officially as canine infectious tracheobronchitis.

While not a particularly dangerous condition, canine cough is frightening because of the harsh, honking cough it produces that can keep a dog, as well as the dog's owner, up all night every night for days or even weeks. The good news is that that awful cough and those sleepless nights are for the most part preventable with a simple vaccine. In fact, any reputable boarding kennel will mandate that all boarders receive this vaccine. This policy, combined with a commitment to maintaining clean kennel quarters, can effectively prevent the onset and transmission of this frustrating, and highly contagious, condition.

Parasites

Dogs are naturally prone to infestations from a variety of parasites, both internal and external. The first step toward preventing such infestations is to know your enemy.

External parasites. On the external front, *fleas* and *ticks,* the most common external parasites, will gladly take up residence in the mass of white fluff of the Samoyed. While fleas reside in grass, carpet, and virtually every and any material within a dog's environment, ticks lay in wait in many of the wilderness areas often frequented by Samoyeds. The best way to combat fleas and ticks, parasites that live off the blood of their victims, is to institute a sound prevention program that includes treating the animal as well as its environment. Products used for this program must be used only as directed and only with other products with which they are safely compatible. Discuss them with your veterinarian.

Internal parasites. While ticks and fleas rarely cause great medical harm, ticks can transmit disease, such as Lyme disease (which can now be prevented with a vaccine), and fleas can introduce into their victim's systems another parasite, an internal parasite, the *tapeworm.* You will know instantly that a tapeworm has taken up residence in your dog's intestine when you spot small ricelike segments around the animal's anus or in its feces. In this case, a trip to the veterinarian for treatment is in order.

Other internal worms, such as *hookworms, roundworms,* and *whipworms,* which share the tapeworm's penchant for an intestinal home, can be more difficult to detect with the naked eye. It is thus wise to have the veterinarian check a fecal sample from your dog every six months just to be sure it is free of these pests. No one wants to think that a beloved pet is hosting an infestation of worms, typically picked up from the fecal material of an infested dog or via an infected mother's milk to her puppies, but should this occur, most infestations can be cleared up quickly and easily with safe and effective prescription medications available from the veterinarian.

Though an adult dog may suffer no serious ill effects from a worm infestation, this is not true of young puppies. A heavy infestation of worms in a puppy's system can lead to severe, even fatal, problems. Roundworms, for example, in addition to causing their young victim great pain and discomfort, can ultimately cause pneumonia should they infiltrate the lungs, while a population of bloodsucking whipworms can cause a potentially fatal case of anemia in so young and physically defenseless an animal. Even a pup from a topnotch breeding program should be tested for worms on its first visit to the veterinarian. If the fecal test results come back positive, the doctor can prescribe the correct dewormer and stop the infestation before it undermines the pup's health.

The *heartworm* is another potentially devastating parasite that typically chooses the dog as its victim. Carried by mosquitoes, heartworm larvae begin their infestation in the dog's circulatory system, ultimately taking up residence in the heart, where they mature and eventually kill their host. Treatment is almost as dangerous as the infestation itself, so doing everything possible to prevent heartworm disease is well worth the effort and expense.

The heartworm prevention program begins with a blood test to determine that the dog has not already been infested by heartworms (the test should be repeated annually thereafter). If the blood is clear, the veterinarian will prescribe an oral preventive medication to be administered to the dog once a month. This simple medication can prevent weeks or even months of pain and suffering for both the dog and its owner—and perhaps save the animal's life.

Parvovirus/Coronavirus

One of the most common diseases to affect the canine species is parvovirus. It's a strong possibility that a dog who is suddenly lethargic, uninterested in eating, is feverish, and has diarrhea possibly laced with blood may be suffering from this viral illness of the intestinal tract. Without treatment, this disease can claim its victim's life.

Especially in danger are young puppies and old or sick dogs, but even a young healthy adult can succumb to parvo's effects. Pre-infection health is critical. The only treatment is supportive fluid therapy designed to prevent dehydration and support the body's own immune system and its attempts to conquer the infection.

In most cases the patient must be hospitalized for this treatment. It will then be several days before the dog exhibits the telltale signs that it is on the mend—an improved demeanor and the ability to eat and drink on its own. Prevention of this devastating illness includes a full series of vaccinations during puppyhood and beyond, a commitment to cleanliness in the dog's environment, and, if at all possible, keeping a healthy dog away from the possibly infected feces of other dogs.

Coronavirus is also a viral infection of the intestines, though it is not as severe as parvovirus and is less likely to claim its victims' lives. Nevertheless, one never knows if the signs a dog is exhibiting are those of parvo or corona, so seeking veterinary attention is critical no matter what the cause. In the meantime, vaccines should be administered for corona just as diligently as those for parvo.

Urinary Tract Disorders

As the average canine lifespan has increased, so has the species' susceptibility to various painful, and often life-threatening disorders of the urinary tract. Included among these are bladder infections, kidney disease, and bladder stones, all of which require immediate veterinary attention.

If you spot blood in your dog's urine, or notice that your pet has suddenly begun to drink and urinate more than ever before, or it seems to strain painfully to urinate, you have legitimate reason to call the veterinarian. Through various tests, he or she can diagnose the problem and prescribe a course of treatment that may involve dietary management, medication, and/or surgery. As with any canine illness, the sooner treatment of a urinary problem begins, the better chance the dog can carry on with a normal, healthy, not to mention comfortable, life for many years to come.

Emergency Action

With a dog as robust and active as the Samoyed, a dog bred for life in the great outdoors, it is only common sense to expect that one day such a dog will be in need of emergency first aid care—and it is only wise for the owner to be well prepared for that possibility.

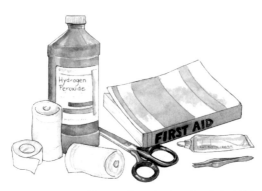

Assemble a well-stocked canine first aid kit before you embark on big adventures with the active Samoyed.

Preparation for Emergencies

Preparation includes not only familiarizing oneself with the procedures of dealing with bleeding wounds, shock, and the like, but also in collecting the supplies that will help ensure that the patient gets to the veterinarian as soon as possible for professional care. The third component to the successful practice of first aid is to remain calm. Your ability to keep your head in a life-threatening situation could save your dog's life.

Proper first aid begins, of course, with a well-stocked first aid kit. This kit should contain the following items:

- gauze pads and rolls in various sizes
- adhesive tape
- antibiotic ointment
- clean towels and blankets
- scissors
- snakebite kit
- hydrogen peroxide
- antiseptic solution
- tweezers
- muzzle (a commercially available leather muzzle or a long strip of soft material such as cotton bandage or nylon stockings that can be twisted into a muzzle)
- tincture of iodine
- canine first aid guide

With these supplies on hand, the Sammy owner may face any new adventure, confident that he or she is prepared for whatever that adventure holds.

Artificial Respiration

A dog that has stopped breathing may be resuscitated with artificial respiration. Keep in mind, however, that a lack of breathing may occur in tandem with, or lead to, cardiac arrest, so before attempting to get the dog breathing again, take the animal's pulse first using these steps:

1. Lay the dog down and lift its hind leg up to reveal the groin area.

2. Tucked into the crease inside the hind leg, where the leg attaches to the body in the groin region, is the femoral artery. Place two fingertips in this region and press gently for the pulse. If you feel a pulse (which averages about 60 to 150 beats per minute in a healthy dog at rest), carry on with artificial respiration. If you do not, you must perform artificial respiration alternately with cardiopulmonary resuscitation (see page 86).

3. To perform artificial respiration, begin by laying the dog on its right side. Extend its head out, open its mouth, and look for items that may be obstructing its breathing, such as a chunk of bone or a small ball. If possible, remove the item.

4. Now close the dog's mouth and hold it closed with your hand. Lean over and open your mouth over the dog's nose, creating a seal by which the only route for air into the dog's lungs is through its nose.

To take your dog's pulse (an important step when performing artificial respiration and CPR), place two fingertips at the crease inside the dog's hind leg where the leg joins with the body in the groin area. A healthy canine pulse is 60 to 150 beats per minute.

5. Breathe five or six times into the dog's nose (small, shallow breaths for Samoyed puppies, longer, deeper breaths for adult dogs).

6. Check to make sure the animal's chest expands each time you breathe; with a dog as heavily coated as the Samoyed, you may need to place a hand on the rib cage to make sure.

7. As long as the dog fails to breathe on its own, perform artificial respiration at about 20 breaths per minute.

8. After about 10 minutes with no success, you may assume the dog has expired.

Cardiopulmonary Resuscitation (CPR)

As with humans, cardiopulmonary resuscitation (CPR) can be performed on a dog whose heart has stopped beating and that thus has no pulse (see instructions on taking the pulse in the section on artificial respiration, page 85). As was noted in the artificial respiration section, a dog that has suffered from cardiac arrest may also stop breathing. If so, CPR must be performed alternately with artificial respiration to keep oxygen in the animal's system and to get the heart beating again. In this case, CPR alone will have no affect on the dog.

To perform CPR:

1. Lay the dog on its right side. If your subject is a puppy, wrap your hand around the puppy's rib cage, your left thumb on the rib area beneath the puppy's left elbow, the remaining fingers of your left hand beneath the puppy. If you are working with an adult dog, place both hands, one hand on top of the other, on the rib area at the dog's left elbow.

2. Now work to compress the chest, either by squeezing the puppy's chest with your fingers, or exerting pressure in a downward motion on the adult. Compress the chest rapidly, at a rate of about 100 compressions per minute. Take a break after every 30 seconds to see if the pulse and heartbeat (and, if necessary, the dog's breathing) have resumed. If after 10 minutes they have not, they are probably not going to.

3. If you do resuscitate the dog, get the animal to the veterinarian as soon as possible for follow-up care (you may have to continue administering CPR along the way—while someone else drives, of course).

Emergency Situations

Bleeding Wounds

A most common—and frightening—condition a dog owner is likely to confront is the bleeding wound. Whether the wound is as minor as a small cut on a paw pad, or as critical as a deep laceration on a hind leg, the goal is to stop the bleeding, and, in severe cases, get the patient to the veterinarian for life-saving follow-up care as quickly as possible.

Some bleeding is a positive biological response in that it helps to cleanse the wound of infectious organisms, but excessive blood loss can lead to severe illness or death. While a minor wound without much blood may be cleaned with soap, water, and antiseptic solution (and the incessant licking of the patient), the goal when faced with a severely bleeding wound is to get the flow stopped right away. You can worry about cleanliness later.

1. Fight the natural human inclination to panic at the sight of blood, and concentrate on restraining the dog. Depending on the dog's temperament and condition, you may need to apply a muzzle and wrap the dog securely in a blanket to keep it as still as possible.

2. Cover the wound with a clean towel, gauze pad, or other cloth, and apply firm pressure with your fingers or hands directly to the wounded area. If no cloth or towels are available, apply the pressure directly to the wound with your bare hands.

3. After about 30 seconds, gently remove the pressure and check the wound. If the blood is still flowing, apply pressure for another 30 seconds. If the blood spurts out rather than flows, you are dealing with an arterial wound, which will require five minutes or more of continuous pressure rather than the 30-second intervals.

4. Finally, even if the blood is still flowing, cover the wound with gauze, and wrap the site firmly with a bandage, taking care not to wrap it too tightly. If blood leaks through, keep the original bandaging in place and simply apply a new layer.

5. Continue to keep the dog still, and carry it either in your arms or in a makeshift blanket stretcher to the veterinarian.

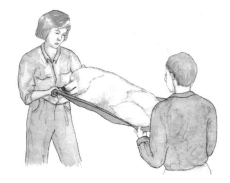

Move a dog suffering from broken bones, shock, or other serious injuries on a stretcher made from a blanket to help ensure that no further injury occurs while transporting the dog to the animal hospital.

Broken Bones

The incidence of bone fractures are common among canine athletes, the most common such fracture being that of a leg. Regardless of where the bone breaks, however, it will result in great pain for the dog. Pain behavior is thus a vivid sign of a broken bone, as is swelling, the dog's refusal to place weight on a leg, limping, or an inability to walk at all.

Broken bones require immediate veterinary attention, but the challenge to the owner is in getting the dog to the doctor for that treatment. If you mishandle the dog, you can easily complicate the problem. The dog must thus be kept as still as possible. This may require applying a muzzle, for the pain may cause even the friendliest Sam to bite, an act for which it certainly cannot be blamed. After muzzling the dog, you may be able to immobilize the fracture site, particularly if it is a leg, by wrapping it gently in a thick folded towel, or by supporting it on a board or other firm surface. Take care not to move the injured area excessively or in a way that could cause increased pain.

Use that same care in transporting the dog to the animal hospital. The safest way to move the animal so as not to damage the fracture site further is to gently lift it onto a blanket or large board, which can then act as a stretcher on which the dog may lie. Carrying the dog in your arms, especially a dog as large as the Samoyed, could cause it further injury.

Burns

Whether the dog finds itself in the path of a wayward camp or kitchen fire, or seals its own ill fate by chewing on electrical cords, the results of canine burns can be quite serious, not to mention painful.

In many cases the Samoyed is somewhat protected from burns by the density and length of its thick coat. When a minor burn does occur, however, resulting in a slight reddening of the skin, the goal is simply to cool the skin and relieve the pain with cold compresses and commercial applications that can numb the burn site.

With diligent attention to its diet, preventive health care, grooming and exercise needs, the Samoyed should live well into its teens and remain very puppy-like in nature for most of its life.

Choking

It is not at all unusual for an active creature like the dog to gobble up with gusto small items—a bone fragment, a rock, a wayward chip of plastic—it finds in the course of a morning walk or play session. Nor is it unusual for one of those items to lodge in the back of the dog's throat and cut off its ability to breathe. In minutes, the dog could be dead.

The signs of a choking dog are not all that different from those of a choking human. The dog may open its mouth helplessly and attempt to vomit. It may salivate and claw at its mouth with its paws. Eventually it will lapse into unconsciousness. If this occurs, you can try a direct remedy: Extend the dog's head, open its mouth, pull out its tongue, and prop one side of its jaw open with a screwdriver handle or other available object. If the offending article is in view and within reach, you can attempt to remove it with tweezers or a set of pliers (fingers may lodge the item farther into the airway, but they may be all you have available).

The open-mouth direct route is quite dangerous with a conscious dog, that, in its panic, might inadvertently bite the hand of the person attempting to help it. Fortunately there is another method that is safer and often even more effective: the canine version of the Heimlich maneuver. To perform this on a choking dog, stand behind the animal, embrace it in a bear hug in the region just below the ribs. Then squeeze and pull up quickly several times in a row. This act compresses the chest and, if done properly, puffs air out of the lungs, dislodges the item, and clears the airway so the dog can resume its breathing.

Heatstroke

A heavily coated dog that was bred for life in the Arctic is obviously a logical candidate for heatstroke. While

Less common are dogs that survive a confrontation with a large fire, which may not only burn the dog's skin, but also damage the animal internally with its fumes and heat. In more severe cases, including those where a dog has been burned by chemicals or electricity, the owner should douse the burn in cold water and compresses, cover the burn with a clean cloth or bandage, and get the dog to the veterinarian as soon as possible for proper treatment and attention to any possible unseen internal damage.

Samoyeds can exist nicely in regions where the temperature does not necessarily dip into the negative realms, this dog, or any dog, for that matter, does require special care to ensure that it is not subjected to conditions that can lead to heatstroke and death.

A dog that has been left in a car with the windows cracked on even a mildly warm day, or is left in the sun with no shelter, or is exercised during the high heat of a summer day, may respond to such conditions with excessive panting, panic, and perhaps an inability to stand up. This dog is suffering from heatstroke and must be cooled down and transported to the veterinarian's office immediately.

Cooling does not mean submerging the dog in ice water, as this too will shock the body. Rather, cooling must occur gradually, preferably by immersing the dog in a tub of *cool* (not cold) water, moving it out of the direct sunlight (preferably into an air-conditioned house), and encouraging it to drink, in small amounts at first, fresh cool water.

Heatstroke is easily preventable. Leave the dog at home on warm days when you will be running errands that require the animal to be left in the car. If you cannot bring the dog into an air-conditioned home, make sure that in its outdoor domicile it will have constant access to fresh cool water and shade (even as the sun moves across the sky). And finally, schedule summertime play and exercise sessions for the cooler times of the day.

Poisoning

There is no generalized remedy for poisoning, as dogs can be poisoned by a variety of materials, each of which requires specialized modes of treatment. Inducing a dog to vomit, for example, may be appropriate for an animal that has ingested a bottle of sweet-tasting baby aspirin, but if you employ this method for a dog that has ingested acid, the dog will probably not survive.

The symptoms of poisoning, too, can vary, a further challenge considering that sometimes a dog is poisoned unbeknownst to its owner by an unknown substance. When a dog appears restless, breathes rapidly, loses consciousness, behaves in an uncharacteristic hyperactive or depressed manner, loses muscle control (often manifested in inappropriate defecation or urination), or is having seizures, poisoning may be the cause.

The best remedy for poisoning is to prevent it from occurring in the first place by keeping potential poisons out of the reach of the curious Sam. It is also wise, just in case the worst does occur, to keep the telephone numbers posted by the telephone of both the veterinarian and the local poison control center. Time is critical for a poisoned dog's survival, and simply having the numbers handy could shave those precious minutes that stand between the animal's life and death.

Shock

Shock is the body's response to such physical traumas as massive blood loss and broken bones. A Samoyed, for example, that has just been hit by a car, may be suddenly weakened internally and become uncharacteristically quiet, refusing to rise from a prone position. Its pulse will be rapid but weak, its gums pale, its breathing shallow, its body temperature dangerously low. Without proper attention, this dog could soon lapse into a coma and die.

In the event of shock, immediate veterinary care is imperative. If this is not possible at the moment, however, your job is to keep the animal warm, calm, and comfortable. You can accomplish this by wrapping the dog

Even the older Samoyed needs its daily walks, which keep the dog both physically and mentally spry.

in blankets and even employing a heating pad if available (do not apply the pad directly to the dog's body; wrap it in a towel or other type of material). Any bleeding must be controlled, too, as this is a common cause of shock. Then do all you can to get the dog to the animal hospital, for most causes of shock require aggressive medical care that only the veterinarian can provide.

Enjoying the Older Samoyed

It is said that there is no greater companion on this earth than the aging Samoyed. As the Samoyed progresses in years, the gusto with which it grasps every element of everyday life is slowly dominated by its passion for the human species and its desire

to revel in our company. Those who have lived with such a creature understand how the bond between Sam and owner can grow even stronger during this time, and most will do anything in their power to ensure their dogs will live just as long, and just as comfortably, as they possibly can.

With proper care, diet, and exercise, the Samoyed should live well into its teens, and remain physically healthy and active, as well. Of course, things will change a bit. The dog will probably begin to sleep more than it did in its youth. Not to worry; enjoy the peaceful companionship. After age seven or eight, it is also wise to take the dog to the veterinarian twice a year for routine examinations, now geriatric visits, which enable the doctor to detect, through blood tests and urinalyses, any budding age-related medical problems that might be halted in their early stages.

Pay special attention to the older dog's diet, as well. Though you might feel compelled to indulge your pet with inappropriate treats that you believe will brighten its later years, keep in mind that obesity can contribute to a variety of age-related problems, plus the older dog may be especially prone to gastric upset, which is unpleasant at any age.

It is not unusual for a dog to lose its hearing in its later years, a development that is easily accommodated by teaching the dog hand signal commands when it is young. The dog's sight may diminish, as well. This is no tragedy as long as you are sensitive to your pet's new navigational impediment and work to bolster its confidence by keeping the objects in its environment in one place, and making sure the dog is always on leash when you are out and about.

Remember, too, that your aging friend, though now older and slower, must not be relegated to a strict couch potato existence. Even at a ripe old age, the Samoyed requires moderate exercise, and you can provide this simply by taking your pet out on daily walks. Walking is ideal for the senior Sam because it addresses the whole animal. It exercises the dog's muscles, limbers up its joints, keeps the digestive tract running smoothly, and stimulates the dog's mind with all the sights and sounds of the world beyond its front door. There is then nothing sweeter than returning home and spending the remainder of the evening in the company of a snoozing, and very contented senior citizen Sam.

Veteran Samoyed owners understand the special bond that can exist between the aging Sam and its family.

Good-bye, Old Friend

It is inevitable. No matter how vigilant we are in fostering our dogs' health, no matter how devoted we are to grooming, exercise, diet, and companionship, the fact remains that we will most likely outlive our dogs. Yes, dogs are now living longer than ever before, but they just don't live long enough.

What makes this issue even more difficult is that often the owner must make the devastating decision of when a beloved pet's life should come to an end. Indeed, some dogs meet untimely deaths from accidents or illness, while others, at an elderly age, pass on peacefully in their sleep. But at one time or another, every individual who chooses to spend his or her life with dogs will be faced with the euthanasia decision. The guilt can be unbearable, even when the dog is so ill and/or in pain that you can see in the animal's eyes the understanding that the time has come. A single painless injection will bring the dog peace, but that doesn't make the decision any easier.

Regardless of how the end comes, and the great sadness in the aftermath, most dog owners agree that the joy and fulfillment of living with one of these special souls far outweigh the tragedy when they are no longer a part of our families. Losing a beloved pet, in this case a Samoyed whom you cannot imagine living without, spawns a pain as genuine as that from losing any family member. Although the animal is gone, you still see a great puff of white fluff out of the corner of your eye in the living room. You still end each evening feeling compelled to take the dog out one more time before you go to bed. It can take weeks, or even months, before the pain of these instincts begins to subside. Yet through it all, you must allow yourself to grieve.

Ignore those who, in their misguided efforts to ease your pain, claim that "it's only a dog," and be realistic about deciding when to bring a new dog into the house. That is a personal choice. Some people are driven to get a new dog right away; others prefer some time alone to grieve before jumping in again to so great a commitment. Honor your own heart and follow whichever path is right for you.

While it is heartbreaking to experience the death of a trusted Samoyed family member, the joy these animals bring to our lives far outweighs the pain of losing that beloved companion.

In the meantime, celebrate the dog you have lost. Share your feelings and your fond remembrances with fellow pet-owning friends, or even seek out pet-loss support groups, which are growing in popularity and acceptance. Then, when you are ready to invite another dog into your life, don't be surprised if you find yourself looking for another Samoyed. People who have lived with this breed once, typically find it impossible to change the habit. But even if you do choose a new Samoyed family member, respect your new pet for who it is. Every dog is unique. Your new pet will not be a clone of your first, but it will bring into your home a whole new set of quirks, a whole new reason to laugh and to love, a whole new collection of memories. Together you will write a new chapter in the lovely living history of the Samoyed.

The Samoyed's Active Lifestyle

Mind and Heart

It should be obvious by now that the moment you invite a Samoyed in to share your home and hearth, your life as you know it will never again be the same. This dog with Christmas both on its face and in its soul will barge in, take hold of the family, and do all it can to ensure that from that day forward, no one is ever bored, sad, lonely, or depressed.

In exchange for its spiritual guidance, there is much the dog's owners must do to foster their pet's continued health and well-being. Yes, we're back to that pesky exercise issue again, which simply cannot be ignored. Consummate athlete that it is, the Sammy's need for activity is almost equal to what it requires in love and attention. The bonus, of course, is that the dog's family members will also benefit from daily exercise of some kind, so in the long run, everybody wins.

Exercise for the athletic Sam is more than simply a means by which its muscles may be strengthened, its energy expended. Ever curious, vibrant, and alive, the Sammy mind, the product of thousands of years of nomadic travels and a respected position in the family, must be exercised just as vigorously as its muscles.

A Samoyed (or any dog, for that matter) cannot be simply turned out into the backyard and be expected to get all the activity it requires by sniffing around in the grass, snoozing in the shade, and running back and forth like a polar bear in a cage from one side of the yard to the other. No, the Sammy requires far more demanding challenges. Beyond that backyard fence lies a world of wonderful sights, sounds, and scents—as well as minions of potentially adoring fans to which the smiling Sam may bestow its light. No healthy self-respecting Samoyed can resist exploration of that world, nor should it be expected to. Indeed, such stimulation is a vital component to the long and healthy lifestyle that is this dog's birthright.

So, if your goal is to provide your dog with the most fulfilling life possible, then a commitment to activity is a road you must travel together from the very start. Of course this commitment

A Samoyed is happiest in mind and healthiest in body if it is offered ample time out and about with its family.

is bound to come more naturally to the dog at times than it is to its human partner, but when you begin to feel like skipping today's walk or this weekend's hike, look over at your dog, take note of its smiling, expectant face that can be a most enticing, most encouraging magnet, and remember why you got into this whole crazy relationship in the first place. Let your Sam be your guide; it's good at that. What you will discover along the way is not only a healthy dog that is with you for many years to come, but a dog that is a better pet, as well. The dog that is nourished in both mind and body is destined to be content, well-adjusted, and even more deeply bonded to its clan. It has lived according to this equation for a very long time.

Proper Conditioning

Common sense will tell you that any type of activity or exercise regimen will succeed only if it is preceded by a sound conditioning program. Even the natural athlete that is the Samoyed must be prepared properly for the activities in which you both expect it to participate, so start early and progress gradually.

The Samoyed's first forays into an active lifestyle actually begin at home during the young puppy's formative weeks and months. Though young pups require much more sleep than do their older counterparts, their waking hours are filled with high-energy antics, exploring nooks and crannies of the household, pouncing on and chewing up tennis shoes or whatever else its owners carelessly leave within its reach, chasing the kids down the hall, and trying its paws at its first games of fetch. When you witness such activities, you'll quickly understand just why puppies require so much more sleep and so much energy from their food.

While most Sammies will fare well with nice long daily walks, the optimum lifestyle for this dog includes additional activities rooted in the ancient callings of their breed. If, for example, you have decided to supplement those daily walks with dog-assisted jogging, in-line skating, or hiking, you will need to build up to that gradually. To safeguard and foster your pet's health, first have the dog examined by the veterinarian to determine that yes, this dog is up to the challenge. Depending on the type and extent of activity you are planning, the veterinarian, in addition to examining the dog for its fitness, may also prescribe nutritional supplements or a high-energy diet for the dog (although this is usually only necessary if the dog will be trained for serious sledding or weight-pulling). He or she may also recommend various training exercises that will help keep it limber and safe from pulled muscles or other painful side effects of exercise.

Once the veterinarian has proclaimed that the dog is up to the new challenge in leg, hip, heart, and lung, view that as the go-ahead to begin introducing the dog to the increased physical demands of its new activity. Do this incrementally, beginning with, say, a half-mile jog for the first couple of days, gradually lengthening the distance every few days as the dog becomes stronger so as not to overtax the animal's system or cause painful muscle strain. You must hold the dog to this schedule, however, for as willing to please as this breed is, and as anxious it is to participate in new adventures, it will unwittingly forge ahead even if it is not yet physically prepared to do so.

In proceeding with this mission, keep climate in mind, as well. While activity in winter weather will be heaven to this dog of the Arctic (and perhaps prove to be more of a challenge to its thin-skinned, essentially hairless, human partners), the birth of spring will naturally inspire you to increase your joint daily exercise program. Yet, warmer, more humid weather can become increasingly oppressive to a lushly coated Samoyed that is giving its all to do your bidding. Be sensitive to your dog's needs. Restrict vigorous activity to the cooler times of the day, beware of hot pavement that can burn even the tough pads of the Samoyed's paws, and watch for the telltale signs—shallow breathing, excessive salivation, pale gums, and/or a wobbly gait—that could indicate pending heatstroke (see Heatstroke, page 88). Make sure, too, that winter or summer, the dog has constant access to fresh, cool water.

A Commitment to Action

While the Samoyed is an ancient sled dog of Arctic origin, do not allow this fact to intimidate you and hinder your ability to provide the dog with what it needs in the way of activity. Snow is not an imperative; this dog will be happy in a variety of activities especially if the entire family is involved.

Walking

Perhaps the easiest, most natural, most traditional activity for Sammy and owner is the age-old one of walking the dog. Just pull out the leash, and the tailspins your dog will perform in response are all you need to convince you that a walk will please your pup to no end. Indeed, a simple walk of at least 30 minutes in duration twice a day, will exercise the dog's muscles and joints, expand the performance of its lungs and heart, and stimulate its mind all at the same time—and it will do the same for you.

One rule of thumb to observe religiously, however, is to make sure that when you walk, the dog remains on leash (which in most communities is the law). Although they are not as inclined to bolt as are their Siberian Husky cousins, Samoyeds are sled dogs with a propensity to pull, forge ahead, and explore new environs—compulsions made all the easier when the dog is running loose. Do not underestimate this ancient calling. the simple leash, coupled with a little training, will counteract the inherent danger in this instinct, and prevent the heartbreak of a lost dog.

Way of walking. Keep an open mind about your dog's particular mode of walking. While the perfect *heel* may be the ideal, that practice does not afford the dog as much exercise as it should get from a vigorous walk. You do not, of course, want the dog to pull your arm out of its socket, which it may be inclined to do inadvertently when it mistakes the leash for a sledding harness (a tendency that for some dogs can be remedied with an H-shaped harness or a correctly used head halter). But a dog that walks loosely on the leash and is allowed to sniff the grass, greet passersby, and visit with other dogs will receive a far more effective workout of both mind and body than will the dog that must remain glued to your side, walking in time to the rhythm of your heels like an automaton.

Walking is the ideal, for it is low-impact and eye-opening and offers both you and the dog the opportunity to meet new friends at every turn. It is also an activity in which you both may—and should—participate together well into the dog's old age. Even an older dog loves its walks, and keeping to the routine will help the elderly Sam remain healthier in body and younger at heart for years to come.

Cleaning up. In addition to making walking a pleasant part of the daily

The good old-fashioned activity of walking the dog helps exercise the curious Samoyed—and its owner.

Whether the youngster is destined to be a suburban companion or the member of a recreational dog-sled team, introduction to daily activity should begin during puppyhood.

routine, you must also commit to practicing good public relations. In other words, never leave home without a pooper-scooper or cleanup bags to pick up the souvenirs your dog will inevitably leave behind (bring extra bags, too, to offer politely to other dog owners you encounter who have conveniently "forgotten" supplies of their own). Cleaning up after one's dog is not only common decency, but it is a critical component of responsible dog ownership, helping to ensure that dogs will continue to be welcome wherever they wish to travel with their trusted owners.

Hiking

So you have mastered the fine art of walking, but would like to carry it a step further. Hiking is that logical step. While you may enjoy walking in your neighborhood, a local beach, or the park on the weekdays, perhaps expanding your forays into the great outdoors to the countryside on the weekends will help satisfy your desire to explore even wider environs with your nature-loving Sam. Summer or winter, such explorations are natural callings for the Samoyed.

While very little, if any, formal training is required to introduce the Samoyed to hiking, a bit of extra preparation on your part is in order. Whether you will be hiking for half a day or an entire weekend, you must make sure to bring ample supplies for your dog: food, water, healthy treats, bedding, and a first aid kit. You may even have the dog carry its own supplies in a properly fitted dog pack (a special backpack for dogs available at specialty stores and by mail order). Carrying its own supplies also comes naturally to the Samoyed, assuming of course that you have introduced the dog to the pack long before the big event. Train the dog first to wear the pack, then accustom it to the sensation of weight in the pack (no more than 25 percent of the dog's weight). The dog will thus not only enjoy the wilderness exploration, but also feel that it is making a valuable contribution to the activity.

Make sure that when venturing into uncharted territory (and familiar ground, too), the dog wears its collar and a current identification tag. Keep the dog on leash at all times, and don't allow it to chase or in any way harass wildlife, which is the fastest way to raise the ire of those critical of dogs on wilderness trails, an issue that has garnered more and more debate these days. Observing the rules and respecting the natural environment and other hikers, will help to ensure that dogs will continue to enjoy access to potentially sensitive areas.

When hiking with a Samoyed, the properly trained and conditioned dog will be honored to pack in its own supplies.

Born to Run

Ancient sled dog that it is, the Samoyed loves to run, and there are several outlets you can use to allow the dog to do just that. The first, of course, is basic jogging. You jog, the dog jogs next to you on leash, and you both, assuming you have both been properly conditioned and the dog trained to match your speed, have a great time.

But if you would like to match the dog's speed rather than the other way around, you can speed up your own pace with wheels—those on a bicycle or those on roller skates. Of course, given the rather precarious position in which you will place yourself when on those wheels, your own safety is in question here. You are entrusting that safety to a dog of incredible power when it gets the mind to run, and you must therefore prepare accordingly.

First, some fundamental training is in order. The most logical canine candidate for accompanying an owner on a bicycle or skates is one that knows how to behave on the leash, that

Whether a Samoyed will be participating in long daily walks or weekend backpacking excursions with its owners, a sound conditioning program is required to protect the dog from overexertion and injury.

Cycling and in-line skating with a Samoyed can be physically rewarding for both dog and owner, but given this dog's sled dog heritage, make sure to wear the appropriate protective gear.

At Home in the Snow

While the contemporary Samoyed can, with proper care, fare well in warmer climes, the snow remains its true home. Activities in a winter wonderland thus spell paradise for this animal that will be in sheer delight with an owner who shares its affinity for the white stuff and makes the effort to satisfy its preprogrammed longings, even if they have to drive a few hours to get there.

Sledding/Mushing

The most natural snow calling for a Samoyed is, or course, pulling a sled. This is actually not as obscure as it may sound in our contemporary world, as the sport has enjoyed an increase in popularity in recent years. Consequently, venues, equipment, and training opportunities have increased, as well.

Internationally known Samoyed enthusiasts Kent and Donna Dannen, who, through their stunning Samoyed photography have elevated the Sammy to a well-deserved art form all its own, refer to their beloved breed as "the station wagon of the sled dog family." While it is not as powerful as the larger Alaskan Malamute, nor as swift as the smaller Siberian Husky, nor as relentless as the Alaskan Husky that takes Iditarod honors year after year, the Samoyed is just right for the fun of recreational mushing.

knows to pay attention to its owner's signals and commands, and that can contain that inherent sled dog desire to pull. Once you trust your dog in these areas, you might try jogging a bit with the animal to see how this inspires its love of speed. Master this, as well as your own skills in cycling and skating, and you're ready to tackle the wheels together.

Even with a trustworthy partner at the other end of the leash, you are wise to outfit yourself with safety in mind. For cycling or skating, wear the necessary helmet and the necessary padding on your elbows, wrists, and knees. Its head can always get the best of even the most trustworthy Sam, so be ready. Should the dog bolt forward in a burst of euphoria, you'll thank your lucky stars and your good common sense that you had the intelligence to use safety gear that can prevent serious injury. You are, after all, pursuing this activity to have fun with your dog, not to make a tragic memory for you both.

To participate in this activity, you will need snow, and, ideally, a minimum of two Samoyeds (three or four is considered ideal). Rounding out the wish list is a sled and proper harnessing (available by mail order and from manufacturers that are typically located in regions known for dogsledding activities). If, however, you don't have snow, you may harness the dogs to a wheeled cart and run them along a little-traveled road or park trail; this is also an excellent exercise for training and conditioning sled dogs and for keeping them in shape during summer.

While it may not take long to get mushing, you should not jump in cold; this is anything but a do-it-yourself vocation. Get acquainted with the sport, and try to get to know people who are involved. First, attend some sledding events (consult the newspaper, local and national kennel clubs, and sled dog breed clubs for information on such events), and, if possible, get a line on instructors who might be able to usher you smoothly and safely into the art of mushing. The unbridled, often startling, power of Samoyeds allowed to pursue their ancient calling can be dangerous in untrained novice hands. A good instructor can help channel the dogs' energy and assist the fledgling musher in learning to contain it with proper sled handling and commands. The result is a fun and extremely addictive activity, during which you will rarely, if ever, feel the cold.

Skijoring

Just as the Samoyed can be trained to run along with its owner on wheels, so can it also learn to do this with an owner on skis. While some may view cross-country skiing as a rather dull, overly strenuous activity, skiing with a dog as your engine is anything but dull or in any way mundane.

Skijoring, as this activity is called, has been compared to waterskiing, but it requires snow instead of water and a dog instead of a boat. It is yet another vigorous athletic activity in which owner and Sammy can participate together, and one that is especially attractive to those who are inspired by the idea of sledding but have access to only one dog. Skijoring may also prove to be friendlier to those who find the notion of mushing a team of Sammies a bit too intimidat-

ing (although skijoring, too, can be daunting in that it involves simply dog and skier, no sled for a buffer).

Critical to your success as a skijorer is, first, your skill at standing up on and maneuvering a pair of cross-country skis. For obvious reasons, only those who have mastered this skill should ever even attempt being pulled across the snow by a dog. If you forego this important step, you run the risk of being pulled off the skis by the power of an unsuspecting Sam that lurches forward and hauls you helplessly across ice, snow, and any other objects that happen to lie in your path. Your dog cannot be held responsible for your own failure to prepare yourself properly and to respect the Samoyed's strength and instincts.

Beyond the basic cross-country training, the same tenets that you employ for wheel-driven activities and sledding apply. Work to master the dog's obedience skills ahead of time and procure the right equipment. Proper harnessing for both dog and skier is critical, and it is available from mail order houses and from manufacturers that specialize in canine athletic equipment, both of which typically advertise in national and specialty dog magazines. Preparation for safe skijoring also involves locating an instructor who will help you and your dog learn the basics of this fascinating sport and encourage you to learn the various skills gradually in flat, uncrowded, uncluttered areas. Like sledding, skijoring should not be viewed as a do-it-yourself activity. You can prevent unnecessary, and potentially serious accidents by enlisting such an individual to help you. Entrusting your well-being to a dog of such power can be dangerous, and you must learn how to control that power. That is not something you can, or should, undertake alone.

(top) Backpacking is a natural activity for the Samoyed.
The properly trained, properly controlled dog will willingly carry
its own supplies in a pack especially designed for dogs.
(above) Pulling a sled is the calling for which the Samoyed
was bred, and one it continues to relish today.
(left) A Samoyed is never too young to be introduced to
the many snow-laden activities in which it may someday
participate.

Formal Activities

The show world is a unique venue all its own. The people are devoted, the dogs lovely, and the competition fierce. While formal showing is not for everyone, it can be paradise for those who love nothing more than basking in the presence of hundreds, sometimes thousands, of purebred dogs. On a more practical note, it also provides would-be Samoyed owners the opportunity to meet a variety of breeders and enthusiasts, and a variety of Sammies, all under one roof. The following are several types of formal show events in which you might find Samoyeds participating, and in which you may wish to participate with your own dog.

The Conformation Show Ring

Often described as beauty pageants for dogs, conformation showing is where dogs are judged on how well they exemplify the standard that governs their breeding. Shown on leash by handlers, the dogs, impeccably groomed and stunningly beautiful, are paraded in front of the judge, who in turn evaluates their conformation and movement. A member of the American Kennel Club Working Group, the Samoyed must not only be beautiful, but must also exhibit a structure and way of moving that convince the judge that it could, in fact, effectively do the work for which it was originally bred. Of course, many, if not most, of the Sammies that earn the championship title never pull a sled, but the structural theory behind the way in which championships are awarded is sound.

In AKC shows, the Samoyeds first compete against each other according to age and gender in the Samoyed breed class. The winner that takes Best of Breed honors then moves on to compete against all the other Best of Breed winners from the Working Group. Needless to say, the Samoyed,

Best in Show honors in the conformation show ring are reserved for those dogs that best exemplify their breed's standard.

with its twinkling eyes, smiling face, and flowing white tresses is always a spectator favorite. The dog that takes Best of Group in the Working Group then moves on to compete against the other Best of Group winners, one of which will be chosen Best in Show.

Dogs that reach these levels, were essentially born for this vocation; they truly love to strut their stuff for the applause, and it shows. But not every

The conformation dog show offers an ideal opportunity for prospective Sammy owners to meet a variety of well-bred Samoyeds and their breeders all in one location.

dog possesses this quality, and not every dog is an appropriate candidate for conformation showing. In fact, most are not. Most dogs are not graced with just the right angle in the shoulder or just the right length of back and curl of tail to qualify for championship status, but this in no way diminishes the nonchampion Sam's qualities as a pet.

If conformation showing is an activity that interests you, think about this before you choose a particular Samoyed for a pet. Discuss it with the breeder—a reputable one, we hope—and have him or her help you choose a puppy that promises to be of show quality. Most breeders will gladly mentor a show world fledgling who purchases a show-quality puppy, in the hope that that puppy will go on and add its own illustrious contributions to its home kennel's name. If, on the other hand, you are simply looking for a pet, remember that this dog is just as valuable as its show brethren—it is just destined for a different type of lifestyle. Companion is a word even more dazzling than champion, and there are plenty of other formal and informal activities in which pet-quality Sammies can participate and claim accolades of their own.

The Sammy in Obedience

Theoretically, obedience competition is an event in which virtually any AKC-registered dog, regardless of conformation, can participate, but if you choose to pursue an obedience championship with a Samoyed, well, just don't be disappointed if the dog doesn't live up to your expectations. It's not, as we have seen, that the dog is unable to learn the commands or is anyway dim in the head. Oh, no. This dog is smart as a whip and can, if it feels so inclined and finds its lessons interesting, learn those commands in a flash, as well as make up many of

its own moves in the process. It's just that sometimes the Sammy simply doesn't feel like obeying, that's all. And when this happens in the obedience show ring, the dog in question will not be taking home any ribbons.

The lack of obedience awards on a given day is something the Samoyed owner must accept with a good nature. With the appropriate sense of humor at the ready—one equal to that of the dog—accepting this should prove no great challenge. Many a Sammy owner has been through it. They practice, practice, practice for months and months and months. The dog has the commands down cold. They arrive at the show, sit at the ready with a line of other dogs, and when the first command is sent the Sam's way, the dog just sits and looks around. It looks from side to side, it looks up at the sky, perhaps watching a passing airplane, then it trots off to greet some children on a nearby swing. Once you get over the notion that your dog has suffered an acute onset of deafness in the past half hour, you realize that the Sammy sense of humor has struck again.

This is not to say that Sammies never reap obedience honors. They can and they do. It's just that they might tend to grow bored with the repetitive exercises and with the competitions themselves; consequently, the Sammies in the group are not typically the dogs you see earning their advanced obedience stripes.

Nevertheless, competition can be fun when pursued with the right perspective, and training of any kind is always valuable, both in what it teaches the dog and in the profound effect it has on the bond between the dog and its owner. In obedience competitions, which are typically sanctioned by either the American Kennel Club or the United Kennel Club and held in conjunction with large all-breed conformation shows, the dog is asked to obey various commands, the complexity determined by the class in which the dog is competing.

Obedience allows dog and owner to pursue a shared goal together, the camaraderie between the pair growing deeper and deeper with every training session, every competition. No ribbons or trophies can replace the value of that bond and the affection with which the Samoyed holds its family.

Pulling Its Own Weight

Most of us have read accounts of Alaskan sled dogs in weight-pulling competitions in the legendary tales of Jack London, and most of us, given the rough treatment of the dogs in many of those tales, would hardly consider this an acceptable calling for a beloved Samoyed pet. But times have changed since prospectors flocked to Alaska and the Yukon to seek gold and to spend their idle hours exploiting their dogs' muscles. In contemporary times, weight pulling is actually a very civilized activity, offering Samoyeds and their owners yet another goal to pursue in a dynamic Samoyed/human partnership.

Most of these contests are sponsored by the International Weight Pull Association, offering dogs of all breeds and mixes of breeds the opportunity to make their owners proud. Dogs of all sizes and weights may participate, and the various weight classes are designed accordingly. Regardless of class, the dogs are asked to pull either wheeled carts or sleds of various weights (depending on the specific weight classes) for specified distances in prescribed time limits. Given the Samoyed's natural inclination to pull, this is a popular activity for this particular breed.

Of course a full-time commitment to conditioning and training on the part of the owner—the coaching end of the team—is critical to this activity. Once the dog has received the veterinarian's stamp of approval to pursue weight pulling, the animal must be trained carefully, its strength built gradually over time so as to prevent injury and muscle strain. The dog and its owner also must learn to communicate, the dog learning to find inspiration in the owner's encouraging words, the owner understanding and respecting that when the dog sits or stands still, whether in practice or competition, the animal is offering the universal signal that it has finished working for the day.

Weight-pulling participants, both human and canine alike, are likely to find that this activity can be quite addictive. An unexpected bonus that invariably emerges is the owner's realization that his or her bond with the dog has deepened immeasurably as the two have worked together. Weight pulling is not for every owner or for every Sam, but the bonds that build between those that pursue it can be beautiful, as well as inspiring, both to witness and to experience.

The Joy of Agility

No discussion of formal canine show activities would be complete without a nod to agility, one of the fastest growing sports in the dog world. Attend an all-breed conformation show, and wherever you see a large group of spectators gathered away from the traditional judging area, it's a safe bet you have found the agility competition.

An enjoyable, undeniably democratic event usually held in conjunction with larger conformation shows, agility showcases a dog's ability to traverse a cleverly designed course of obstacles with enthusiastic coaching from its owner. Not only is agility fun to watch—and immensely enjoyable for the participating dogs—but it is also

Samoyeds rarely break records in obedience trials, but they can learn to enjoy the activity if you keep the training interesting and free of tedious repetitions.

The growing sport of agility forges a special bond between dog and owner that is strengthened during the time they spend training and competing.

a wonderful conditioning and bonding activity, and a terrific, very active, alternative to more formal showing activities.

In preparing for competition, owner and dog spend a great deal of time together training for shared success in the agility ring, the dog mastering such skills as climbing ladders, running up and down ramps, and crawling through tunnels. As anxious to please as it is, the Samoyed should take quickly to these exciting exercises that promise to satisfy this animal's thirst for activities that are a bit out of the ordinary. In the process, the dog emerges in better shape than it was before it began training, and anxious to run the course again and again.

Traditional Callings

For those who seek to celebrate their Sammy's natural talents and instincts beyond the formal show ring, this, the jack-of-all-trades northern breed, may excel in a variety of other callings as well.

Herding Dogs

Think back to the Samoyed's not-so-humble origins, when it was called upon to participate in just about every aspect of its Siberian people's Arctic existence. One of those was herding reindeer. Now it appears that some of the progeny of those dogs that share our contemporary homes today, despite their separation from Rudolph and his pals for some years now, have retained that herding instinct. In light of this fact, many modern-day owners are respecting that instinct and allowing their dogs to pursue this ancient activity.

While we may probably assume that it's a Sammy that herds Santa's reindeer around the North Pole when the need arises, here in more subarctic realms, the animals in need of herding are sheep, and there are some Samoyeds out there who have proven themselves willing and able to comply. These Sams invariably convey their herding desires to their owners by leaping for joy the moment they first hear a "baa" or catch the distinctive scent of a sheep. As word is spreading throughout the Samoyed community that more and more Samoyeds are successfully competing in herding, more and more are getting involved. Those that succeed tend to be dogs that exhibit a natural interest in sheep or other animals that travel in packs and flocks, and they have a grand old time pursuing that interest, to the delight and amazement of both owners and spectators alike.

Some Samoyeds today exhibit their ancient Arctic herding instincts in organized herding trials.

Assistance Dogs

Also gaining attention these days are Samoyed assistance dogs. Although there are not many of them and their headstrong ways make them more of a challenge to train (treats and consistency are the keys) than the far-more-common, far-more-obedient Golden Retrievers and the like, the Samoyed's charm and dedication have made it a willing, and very lovable, companion to the physically challenged.

Therapy Dogs

A related vocation that is accessible to more Samoyeds, and seems a perfect match for this breed's character, is that of therapy dog. Rarely will you find a dog more welcome in convalescent homes, children's hospitals, rehabilitation centers, and related venues than a smiling Sam that also happens to be a registered therapy dog. Although the Samoyed's size can be intimidating initially to patients, such intimidation is usually short-lived. The breed's legendary unconditional love of people shines brightly and melts even the most frightened soul when

the dog works to ease the pain, fears, and loneliness of people in often sterile, less-than-cozy hospital settings—but the Sammy makes it cozy; the Sammy makes it warm.

The registered therapy dog is well-behaved, gentle, healthy, and calm in disposition. If this is a noble calling you would like to pursue with your dog—and there are few activities with your Samoyed that you will find more rewarding—work on obedience training, socialization, and grooming, and

The sight of a Samoyed herding sheep may be disarming at first, but it is a calling naturally suited to this breed that historically herded reindeer in its Arctic homeland.

Therapy dog work is ideally suited to the Samoyed, a dog that is not only beautiful, but also possesses a universal affection for human beings.

contact one of the many organizations that sponsors and certifies therapy dogs. You will never forget the expressions of gratitude and affection on the faces of troubled people who discover themselves suddenly blessed with the presence of a Samoyed in their midst.

A Hard-Working Companion

Occasionally you run across a dog's official name and notice a string of letters after its long, often unusual, title. This alphabet soup is designed to announce to the world just what the dog has accomplished in its life: obedience titles, therapy work, herding titles, health certifications, etc.

When you see the letters CGC after a Sammy's name, you know you have run across a special dog. These initials tell the world that this dog has earned the status of Canine Good Citizen, as awarded by the American Kennel Club. A relatively new test in the AKC's roster of goals for which dogs may work, the Canine Good Citizen test encourages dog owners to strive for exemplary behavior and socialization in their dogs. At the same time, it helps to further the aim of making dogs welcome in as many

venues, as many public situations, as possible.

To earn those coveted initials after its name a dog must pass a battery of tests designed to test its ability to tolerate the many surprises and obstacles that await it in public life:
• It must exhibit its proficiency in the basic obedience commands.
• It must walk without pulling on the leash.
• It must display an ability to ignore visual and sound distractions.
• It must permit a stranger to pet and brush it (a particular favorite of the Samoyed).

Passing these tests may require some practice ahead of time, but what a grand accomplishment it is to earn this high accolade that rewards dogs for their abilities as companions, which is, after all, the dog's highest calling.

In addition to the more traditional familiar initials that represent excellence in herding, obedience, and the like, Samoyeds may also complete for special awards all their own, awards that celebrate the breed's ancient and very versatile work ethic. The gainfully employed Sammy is a happy Sammy, and working toward these titles will take it to the heights of contentment.

Working Dog Certification Program

The Samoyed Club of America, for one, sponsors what is known as the SCA Working Dog Certification Program, which recognizes Sammies that earn points for their participation in one or more of eight different Sammy vocations. These include:
• sled dog racing
• excursion sledding
• herding
• skijoring
• packing
• weight pulling
• therapy dog work
• a catch-all category for work that does not fall into the other categories,

such as work in television and film and assistance-dog work.

The dog that earns 1,000 points earns the Working Samoyed (WS) title. If it earns 500 more it becomes a Working Samoyed Excellent (WSE). And then there is the ultimate: the Master Working Samoyed (WSXM). This is a dog that has earned 5,000 points in at least four of the eight designated categories.

Organization for the Working Samoyed

Another organization also rewards Samoyeds for their versatility and their love of work. This is the Organization for the Working Samoyed, which each year honors those Samoyeds that excel in sled dog racing, obedience, and weight pulling. This organization also provides members with information on the optimum care of the working Sam, whose needs may be a bit more demanding that one that is not so vigorously employed.

Whether you are working toward one of these illustrious working Samoyed titles or not, the bottom line is that your Sam, any Sam, must have a job and believe that each day it is being called to a respected vocation in your service. That may be pulling a

A position as full-fledged family member is the greatest gift you can offer your pet Samoyed.

sled, competing in obedience, or rounding up sheep, or it may be simply accompanying its family on daily walks and weekend hikes to make sure that they get the exercise they need to remain healthy. Regardless of the dog's calling, whether it is grounded in wilderness exploration or suburban fun, the core of every Sammy's situation is family. And the exalted position of ultimate family companion and member is all any Samoyed asks for.

Useful Addresses and Literature

Organizations
The Samoyed Club of America
Lori Elvera, Corresponding Secretary
3711 Brices Ford Court
Fairfax, VA 22033
www.samoyed.org/Samoyed_Club_of_
   America.html

The Organization for the Working
   Samoyed
Donna Dannen, President
1997 Big Owl Road
Allenspark, CO 80510
www.samoyed.org/ows.html

Samoyed Dogs (Web Site)
www.samoyed.org/
   Offers direct access to sites for the
Samoyed Club of America, the
Organization for the Working
Samoyed, Samoyed Rescue, etc.

SAMFANS
www.samoyed.org/samfans.html
Samoyed Fanciers Internet mailing list

The American Kennel Club
51 Madison Avenue
New York, NY 10010
Customer Service:
(919) 233-9767

The Canadian Kennel Club
89 Skyway Avenue, Suite 100
Etobicoke, Ontario, Canada
M9W 6R4
(416) 675-5511

Health Organizations
The Orthopedic Foundation for
   Animals
2300 Nifong Boulevard
Columbia, MO 65201
(573) 442-0418
www.prodogs.com/chn/ofa/index

The Canine Eye Registration
   Foundation (CERF)
SCC-A
Purdue University
W. Lafayette, IN 47907
(317) 494-8179
www.prodogs.com//chn/cerf/index.htm

Periodicals
*Samoyed Club of America, Inc.
   Bulletin*
681 Poor Boy Ranch Road
Wright City, MO 63390

AKC Gazette
51 Madison Avenue
New York, NY 10010

Dog World
29 N. Wacker Drive
Chicago, IL 60606

Dog Fancy
P.O. Box 6050
Mission Viejo, CA 92690

Mushing Magazine
P.O. Box 149
Ester, AK 99725

Books

Alderton, David, *The Dog Care Manual*. Barron's Educational Series, Inc., Hauppauge, NY, 1986.

Baer, Ted, *Communicating with Your Dog,* Barron's Educational Series, Inc., Hauppauge, NY, 1989.

Baer, Ted, *How to Teach Your Old Dog New Tricks*. Barron's Educational Series, Inc., Hauppauge, NY, 1991.

Campbell, William, *Behavior Problems in Dogs,* American Veterinary Publications, Inc., Goleta, CA, 1992.

Carlson, Delbert G., D.V.M., and Griffin, James M., M.D., *Dog Owner's Home Veterinary Handbook,* Howell Book House, New York, NY, 1992.

Dunbar, Ian, and Bohnenkamp, Gwen, *Behaviour Booklets* (various subjects), Center for Applied Animal Behaviour, Berkeley, CA, 1986.

Frye, Fredric, *First Aid for Your Dog,* Barron's Educational Series, Inc., Hauppauge, NY, 1987.

Ludwig, Gerd. *Fun and Games with Your Dog*. Barron's Educational Series, Inc., Hauppauge, NY, 1996.

Pinney, Chris C., D.V.M. *Caring for Your Older Dog*. Barron's Educational Series, Inc., Hauppauge, NY, 1995.

Pinney, Chris C., D.V.M. *Guide to Home Pet Grooming*. Barron's Educational Series, Inc., Hauppauge, NY, 1991.

Siegal, Mordecai, *UC Davis Book of Dogs,* HarperCollins Publishers, New York, NY, 1995.

Ward, Robert H. and Dolly, *The New Complete Samoyed,* Howell Book House, New York, NY, 1985.

Wrede, Barbara J., *Before You Buy That Puppy*. Barron's Educational Series, Inc., Hauppauge, NY, 1994.

Wrede, Barbara J., *Civilizing Your Puppy,* Barron's Educational Series, Inc., Hauppauge, NY, 1992.

Index

...Samoyed has been bred for hundreds of years as a sled dog and companion. From the breed's first family, the native people of the Arctic, to today's contemporary enthusiasts, all have shared an admiration for the Samoyed's beauty, athleticism, and natural affection for humans.